Paul Klee DRAWINGS

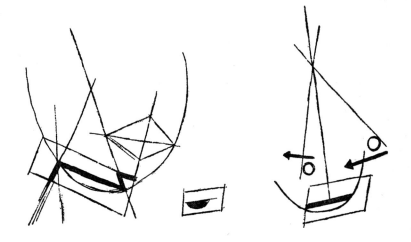

1917/152   Zeichnung zum Unstern der Schiffe

Will Grohmann

Drawings

Harry N. Abrams, Inc., Publishers, New York

On the half-title page: *Constructive Play*   *1927*
Frontispiece: *Drawing for Evil Star of Ships*   *1917*
On this page: *A Good Joke*   *1913*

Library of Congress Catalog Card Number: 60-11598
Milton S. Fox, Editor
Translated from the German by Norbert Guterman
Published 1960 in association with Verlag M. DuMont Schauberg,
Cologne, Germany

1913 84. gute Unterhaltung

Contents

Reproductions in the Text

Plates

Preface

I planned to publish a book on Klee's drawings more than twenty-five years ago, when Klee was still alive. In 1933 I assembled material for a first volume, covering works from 1921 to 1930, but when it was published in 1934, the Gestapo confiscated the edition. It was out of the question to go on with my plans for a second volume, covering drawings from 1930 on. Now, thanks to the interest of the publishing house of M. DuMont Schauberg in Cologne, the original plan for two-volume publication of the drawings is being realized. There will be a second volume, which will contain a catalogue of all of Klee's drawings. Collectors, both public and private, are urged to supply the author with lists of the drawings they own, so that the catalogue may be as complete as possible. The idea is to provide a great many small reproductions, so as to give an ensemble view of what is a truly varied output. Reproduction of every drawing has proved impossible.

I must acknowledge with special gratitude the kindness of Felix Klee and the Klee Foundation in Bern in putting their treasures at my disposal. I wish to thank also the many collectors who have aided me. Their names will be found in the Catalogue of Works Reproduced (page 169).

I believe that the time has come to make accessible Klee's drawings to as wide a public as possible. Reproductions cannot, of course, replace the originals, but in most cases they can give a fairly good idea of Klee's work in the graphic medium. Klee regarded his drawings as highly important, and frequently expressed regret that they were so little appreciated and understood. He was surprised at my temerity in 1925, when I published a first essay on his drawings, for they were as yet known and admired by very few. It is hoped that this volume will widen the circle of admirers, and bring out Klee's remarkable originality in a fresh, though unquestionably basic, aspect of his life and work.

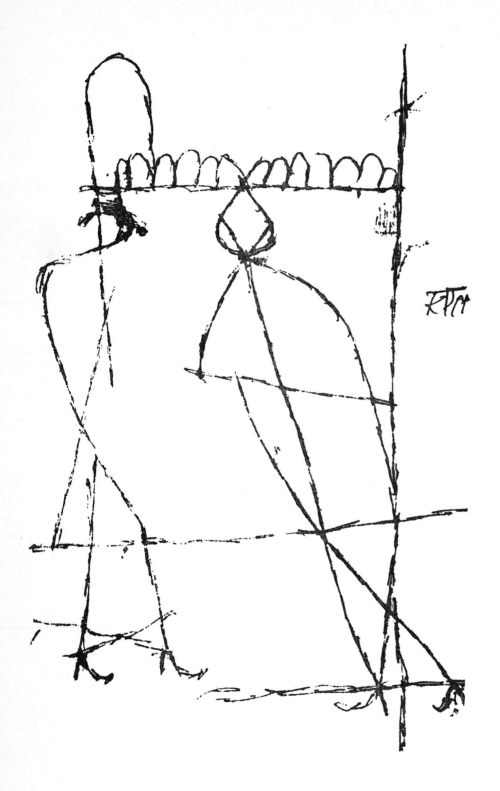

Sketch from Kairouan 1914

8

1 Paul Klee, the Draftsman

Paul Klee produced some 9,000 works, of which nearly 5,000 are drawings*. They constitute the largest graphic output of any twentieth-century artist, and surely one of the most significant. Quite unlike Pablo Picasso, whose drawings have little bearing upon our understanding of his art, Klee always embodies an essential aspect of his artistic inventiveness in his drawings. Klee himself attached great value to them and clung to them as to a sort of personal archive; he gave away or sold very few of them during his lifetime. He preserved them in portfolios arranged year by year right up to 1939. He intended to leave the whole collection to a museum and thought especially of the public Kunstsammlung in Basel as a suitable choice. Had this plan been realized, it would have made the Kunstsammlung unique among museums of modern art. However, during the Second World War the general feeling of insecurity spread even to Switzerland. Klee kept putting off his decision, and after his death—his wife died not long after—a different plan was arrived at. In 1947 the Klee Foundation was organized and attached to the Kunstmuseum in Bern. It owns 2,571 works by Klee, of which 2,250 are drawings. A further 689 drawings are in the possession of the artist's son, Felix Klee, who lives in Bern, and thus nearly 3,000 of Paul Klee's drawings are located in a single city. The rest are scattered all over the world, and it will be no easy task to locate them all.

At the beginning of his career and for some time thereafter Klee felt that he was essentially a draftsman, and that the only way he could ever earn a living as an artist would be by producing illustrations. He devoted himself almost exclusively to making drawings and prints for some years, with only a very few attempts at watercolor before 1914, and very few oils before 1919. Before 1914—i. e., before his trip to Kairouan in Tunisia—his watercolors were far less numerous than his drawings. In 1911 he produced 100 drawings but only 9 watercolors, and it was not until 1914 that the latter began to preponderate over the "monochromes" (111 as against 92). In that year, Klee wrote in his diary: "Color has taken hold of me. No longer do I have to chase after it. I know that it has taken possession of me forever. That is the meaning of this happy moment. Color and I are one. I am a painter."

*The catalogue in Paul Klee's handwriting lists 8,918 works (paintings, watercolors, drawings, prints, and sculptures), including 4,877 drawings. Felix Klee discovered many uncatalogued works among Klee's papers and elsewhere, and was able to add 228 items to his father's list. The total thus comes to 9,146 today, and the number of drawings to 4,966.

Klee was a painter indeed, but drawing was always to remain an essential part of his artistic experiments and intellectual reflections. Everything that caught his interest found its first—and sometimes not only its first—expression in drawing. Occasionally he made drawings after a watercolor or a painting, as though testing the earlier work, or simply to have a sketch of it for his personal archive. In such cases his drawings are always new versions, for he never repeated himself. Even in later years, the output of drawings sometimes outnumbers the works in other mediums. From 1926 on their number steadily mounts; for 1927 we find 210 drawings as against 110 watercolors, while in 1933 the numbers are 336 as against 146, and in 1939 as many as 962 as against 291. During his long illness, as his physical strength declined, it was easier to draw than to cope with paint and canvas. Wishing to record for posterity his last insights and experiences as concisely as possible, by the end of his life he was restricted to the graphic medium as the most economical. In the first five months of 1940, the year of his death, he executed 251 drawings.

The Great Dome 1927

2 Music and the Nature of Form

Shortly before he found himself as a painter in oils, in July, 1918, Klee wrote an essay on drawing for a symposium entitled *Creative Credo*. It seems that he was still giving precedence to drawing: "Since it is so much more likely to lead to abstraction, it is bound to be appreciated in our day. By its very nature it can render the representational element more schematically, in a more magical, more unrepresentational way, and can do so with incomparably greater precision. The more purely graphic our treatment—i. e., the more completely we espouse the fundamental elements of drawing—the less bound are we to a realistic representation of things. . . . Pure art is born when the expression of the formal element and the expression of the formal organism coincide visibly with the spirit of the content." (Quoted from Klee's first version, published by Klipstein and Kornfeld, 1956.)

Klee goes on to explain what he considered to be the formal elements of drawing: dots and linear energies, whether two-dimensional or three-dimensional. As an example of a two-dimensional element, he suggested "an energy traced by a broad-edged pencil without modulation. A three-dimensional element is a vaporous or cloudlike spot of various degrees of intensity made with a full brush." In offering the topographical plan of a "little trip to the land of deeper insight," he describes both lines (and their pictorial meanings as broken lines, undulatory movements, etc.) and more complex formal patterns (such as polyphony, convergence, dynamism). "Some basket weavers on their way home with their cart (the wheel). Among them is a child with funny curls (corkscrew movement)."

However, a work is more than the sum of the elements that make it up: the elements produce the forms, but they are not sacrificed in the process. The idea of Creation is mentioned—right down to his death this idea remained one of the main components of Klee's pictorial thinking. He rejects the distinction between spatial and temporal art, "For space, too, is a temporal concept. . . The state of rest on earth is an accidental inhibition of matter. . . . The pictorial work originates in movement, is itself a record of movement, and is perceived in movement." As early as 1914 he noted in his diary: "Ingres is supposed to have brought order into repose; I should like to bring order into movement, going beyond mere pathos." And at the Bauhaus (1922) Klee formulated his ideas on this matter very precisely: "No work is primarily a product, something that is; it is first and foremost a creation, something in process of being born."

"Formerly artists represented the things they saw all around them . . . today we reveal the relativity [in the edition of 1920 this term was mistakenly printed "reality"] of all things visible." Things visible are for him no more than isolated instances.

There are many other truths still to be discovered. Thus it followed in his thinking that the merely accidental must be "essentialized," its forms brought together and combined either in concrete beings or in abstract things like numbers, so as to produce at last a formal cosmos, one "so closely resembling the Creation that a breath is sufficient to turn an expression of religion or religious feelings into reality."

In this early essay Klee starts from the idea that art does not reproduce visible things, but makes things visible—that art is a metaphor of Creation and is in each particular work an example or instance, just as the terrestrial is an example or instance of the cosmic. "In the highest circle an ultimate mystery stands behind the polyvalence [of pictorial forms], and the flickering light of the intellect is snuffed out."

Never before had anyone analyzed the potentialities of the graphic medium so thoroughly, and Klee never had to correct his essay in later years; he merely added to and further developed what he outlined in 1918. For instance, in a lecture at Jena in 1924, he spoke at greater length about the secrets of his own creative method, about how he was guided by pictorial considerations, but also by observation of nature and life. A work cannot merely reproduce the order the artist discovers in nature, he said on this occasion. Different functions discernible in different elemental realms must lead to conspicuous deviations. Transposition into "the specific dimensions of the pictorial" necessarily entails deformations; nature is reborn, as it were. Thus, according to Klee, the painter can create forms analogous to nature, more highly organized than natural forms, which, as though of their own accord, suggest comparisons with the latter, "according to the association provoked in each case." And it is these associations that induce us to interpret the picture in representational terms. "Now it is looking at me," Klee used to say about a work in progress, once the formal process was sufficiently advanced to make him accept the association. At this point a figure would emerge, whose general appearance and gestures might suggest such a title as *Governess* (page 90) or *Windmill Flowers* (page 109). He intervened "at places still somewhat unsatisfactory" to achieve form, to effect a rebirth of nature.

Klee also kept the viewer in mind: he realized that the viewer may be incapable of reconstructing the artistic processes as such. For this reason, he sets out to explain how it is possible seriously to misunderstand a painter. The viewer starts from the "end forms," while the artist starts at the beginning of the creative process, and "instead of a ready-made natural image" sees "the image of Creation as Genesis, which is alone essential." Thereby "he extends the world-creating act forward in time, endowing Genesis with permanence." The artist replaces mechanical time with ontological time, in which past, present, and future are all present at once. What the eye sees is merely a special instance; Klee as artist tries to go on from this to the primordial image or archetype, to "the primal ground of creation, which holds the secret key to all things." Ten years earlier he had written in his diary: "I cannot be understood in this-worldly terms, for I am just as much at home with the dead and with those who are yet unborn. I am just a bit closer to the heart of Creation than is customary. And yet not—not nearly—close enough."

To progress step by step through all these labors is not all. The finished work is valid only if "it has been wholly realized in formal terms, with the aid of the suitable pictorial techniques," i. e., if the artistic process has been carried to the very end. This idea was the recurrent theme of all his lectures and practical exercises at the Bauhaus, where he examined the origin and nature of the work of art. "We do not aim at form but at function; formalism is form without function." Here he gave examples: "brain, muscles, bones; waterfalls, gears, hammers; active-middle voice-passive." The student must learn how to see behind the façade of appearances, to grasp the thing by its roots. Starting from observation of nature as the *conditio sine qua non* of art, Klee covered all the formal elements of art—the dimensions of line, chiaroscuro, perspective and space, statics and dynamics, structural and individual rhythms, forms of movement. Everything is defined with precision, but "construction is not all." Genius is not industriousness, genius is begetting. The concept of genius must be kept guarded, like "a secret in a locked room." It is the unknown factor. The result: works that deviate from the visual appearance of an object, yet do not, in an essential sense, contradict it.

At the age of forty-five Klee produced the definitive formulation of his views on art. Actually, from his earliest efforts, it was always clear where his insights were leading. As early as 1901 he had noted in his diary: "My mirror takes me right to the heart of things . . . my faces are truer than people's own faces." In 1902 he noted: "To express manysidedness in one word." In 1903 he wrote to his future wife, Lily Stumpf: "Plastic art never has its start in a poetic mood or an idea, but in the construction of one or more figures . . . an idea may be added, but it need not be." In 1904 he wrote: "Then my pencil managed to go off on a few walks that produced some usable motifs." Year by year Klee grew in stature through practice and experience; by 1914 he had caught up with Kandinsky, whose saying, "The work of art becomes the subject," applies to Klee so perfectly that he might have said it himself.

Klee's key insights were obtained from his work in what he thought of as "the richly diversified" graphic medium—drawing. It was from his drawings that the fundamental ideas of the Jena lecture were derived. Klee was indebted to no one else, not even to his friends of the Blaue Reiter, for his ideas on art; with him, everything came out of his own experience. His relation to Cubism was most oblique—to Delaunay, somewhat closer. He admired Kandinsky, but was well aware what different artists they were and continued to be. Kandinsky was trying at first to make the work of art an echo of the real world—later, to oppose the concrete reality of the picture to reality. Klee, for his part, always aimed at a rebirth of reality in the picture. He preferred the term "absolute" to the term "abstract"; according to him, the abstract quality in a work was absolute, and, like the "abstractness" of a piece of music or a poem, was not an attribute of the theoretical structure, but existed in its own right. Abstraction could even serve to bolster reality, so long as the artist strove "to master the conflicting material of life with open senses, to discover its meaning, and at the same time to develop it as fully as possible." In another context he said: "To be an abstract painter is not to abstract from the possibility of comparison with natural appearances, but to release pure pictorial relationships independent of all such comparisons."

In other words, the abstract quality of a picture exists in its own right, as does that of a musical composition. Klee often spoke of music, but, unlike Kandinsky, not in terms of its general effects, but rather in terms of compositional technique. Klee possessed some musical talent; he played the violin for an hour every morning, to prepare himself for work. He envied musicians, saying they have a well-established, thousand-year-old tradition, a secure foundation on which to build. His own ambition was to lay the cornerstone for a system of pictorial harmony, which would be as capable of development as the musical one. In this he was successful.

Bach and Mozart were his formal conscience. He knew the score of *Don Giovanni* bar by bar. It is noteworthy that he always chose classical composers when he wanted musical examples rather than the moderns, although he knew the latter quite well, too. But according to him, no general canon could be built up on the basis of their works. Much as a musician might do, Klee distinguishes between brief and endless melodies, between polyphonic and harmonic compositions, between fugues and sonatas. He thought that painting was richer in polyphonic possibilities than music, because the concept of simultaneity finds a purer embodiment in painting. He did not think it possible to transpose music into painting, but according to him the painter should gain entry to the cosmic realm of polyphonic works and emerge from it transformed. In teaching one of his classes, he used to represent a musical theme pictorially, taking two bars from a Bach three-part invention for this purpose. He would illustrate the dynamics and tonal qualities by lines of varying thickness. Another time he drew pictures to illustrate bars of music. He spoke of simple and complex rhythms, of rhythmic breaks and multiple rhythms, of syncopation, and of ornaments. He even illustrated mirror and crab canon (inversion and retrograde imitation). Musical allusions crop up again and again in the titles of Klee's works: for example, *Fugue in Red, Abstract Trio, Overtones, Bow Stroke*. His use of parallel figurations in such a work as *View of a Mountain Shrine* (page 105) suggests the function of imitation in music; their imbrications, interlockings, and reversals make a kind of fugue. His pictures involving calligraphic symbols look like musical scores, and his horizontal patterns frequently evoke sheets of music paper. Certain small forms—especially S-shaped spirals and banderoles—recur insistently in work after work for a time, like motifs that are gradually being developed into themes. Klee's art is permeated with music, as was his life, for not a day went by that he did not play music and listen to music. No wonder he is a favorite painter among musicians, and had many musician friends, including performers such as Adolf Busch and composers such as Hindemith. He was as good a judge of contemporary composers as of those of the past. He felt a particular affinity with Hindemith, for sharing his own "deep reserve where things of the soul are concerned." He admired the latter's magnificent sense of rhythm and the severity of his harmonies. When he called Carl Maria von Weber the Stravinsky of romanticism, he showed his grasp of modern music.

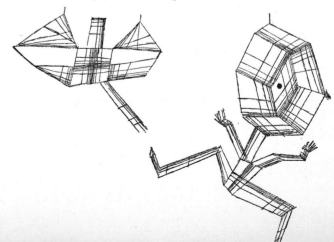

Excitement Before Trip 1927

3   The Role of Titles: Klee as Poet

Because of the titles he gave his works, Klee has frequently been called a poet, and it may be true that in addition to being a painter and a musician he had a gift for poetry. It is not so remarkable that he wrote a number of poems—many painters have done the same—but that he was creative with language. He frequently invented words and figures of speech to fit his pictorial inventions. He gave the name *Beride* to an imaginary country he depicted in a series of drawings. He called one sad-faced figure, *Lomolarm*. Other inventions are a *Chair Animal*, a *Twittering Machine*, *Windmill Flowers* (page 109), and a *Diagram of the Redemption* (page 44). He always titled his pictures after they had been completed; it was always the work itself or some portion of it that suggested the name. This artist's inventiveness did not stop when the picture was finished; then he looked around for a suitable title. Nor was it always easy: Klee was very often driven to go beyond the ordinary resources of the German language.

However, in choosing a title Klee did not just indulge his fancy—he had the viewer in mind. He is trying to explain his intention in the picture. Of course, to call a figurative drawing *Beginning of Winter* (page 169) or a "free" composition *Between Autumn and Winter* (page 136), is deliberately to inject meanings not apparent in the picture. But there is no attempt to mislead; what the title suggests is meant to be helpful, even when it adds something. Since the elements of the drawing indeed suggest that the subject is growth, *Stirrings of Growth* (page 148) seems an eminently fitting title, and yet it is not strictly descriptive. A further poetic connotation of the drawing is invoked, because the pictorial processes are new, and their results are not given in advance. Even in the case of seemingly obvious titles, such as *Façade* (page 96) or *Village Clown* (page 100), the relation between the drawing and the title is by no means self-evident, for the "façade" is not a façade, and the "clown" is not a clown. The titles are "expedients of communication." A picture may be thought of as a suggestion, a hypothesis; then the title is a second hypothesis. The first consists of the totality of the pictorial elements and rests upon the unknown law that governs relations between subject and object—a law Goethe once spoke of. The second implies that the artist stands off at a certain distance from his work, that he has gone beyond it.

In 1911 Klee said that the painter should be a scientist, a philosopher, and a poet, but in later years this did not seem enough. It is very hard to realize just how many fields of knowledge attracted and held him. He read and assimilated a tremendous amount of literature. He could read and understand the Greek tragic poets, for instance, and he adapted their spirit and style to his own (*Experiment for Antigone*, page 138; *For the "Suppliants,"* page 130). He had been interested in contemporary authors as a schoolboy, but in later years read them rarely, preferring the classics, whenever possible in the original. During his years in Munich he was enthusiastic about Voltaire's *Candide;* during his last years in Bern he studied Racine, and *Parsifal* (in the Middle-High German version). He knew Cervantes and Shakespeare, and he loved Goethe. Because Goethe combined scientific thinking with intuition *(Morphologie)*, he felt an affinity with him. He also was drawn to the *Westöstlicher Divan*, which, like Klee's own works, reaches out beyond Europe to the Near East. He did not care to read many books *about* things, but preferred to go directly to the source. He made exceptions for biographies of composers—especially of Bach and Mozart—and for the studies in harmony by Hans Kayser, who was a regular member of the chamber-music groups that met every Wednesday at Klee's house. Kayser's ideas had a very considerable influence on Klee's theory of figuration.

Although he was also a philosopher, he did not enjoy reading philosophical books, but loved to solve problems in mathematics. His lectures on the teaching of art show that he was quite proficient in this field. He could read abstruse scientific books and journals as easily as novels. The ideas he encountered were always adapted to his own needs, and in his practical application of them he rarely followed the letter of the law—he wanted to know the laws only so as to be able to break them in his art. But to the end of his life he was also a faithful student of nature; his powers of observation were amazing, and he often applied them to small things which are usually overlooked, such as clumps of moss, certain woven patterns, pieces of petrified wood, and crystals. He watched the behavior of birds, insects, and snakes, and also studied the people around him more closely than is customary. He noted the comic and the tragic moments alike, and by combining over-all appearance with precise gesture, construction, and graphic expression, he made himself one of the greatest physiognomists of all time (*Portrait of a Scholar*, page 126; *Old Maid*, page 127).

Hardly an area of nature or culture fails to be reflected somewhere in Klee's work: animal life, plant life, geology, weather, physiological or medical processes, and even music and the fine arts. But what makes him "the great realist" of our century is something else: he does not show us the facts themselves, but their successive states or transformations in time and space, their relation to past and future, their fate. Klee could even give pictorial statement to definitions or concepts, as in such drawings as *Frost* (page 137) and *Disgrace* (page 154). He was not conscious of anything remarkable in this gift—the world he lived in seemed to him to include ungraspable elements as well as forgotten or prehistoric ones. He knew that there is a primordial ground of creation, "which holds the secret key to all things." He was thus able to link the remote past with future worlds or other stars.

"My hand is wholly the instrument of some remote power. It is not my intellect that runs the show, but something different, something higher, and more distant—somewhere else. I must have great friends there, bright ones, but somber ones, too."

Klee thought it was important to transform all this into "artistic realities," which add a little breadth to life, and which can make secret things visible. For it is up to the artist "to decide whether he will beget pictures or something else . . . and the kind of picture as well."

Time and again in Klee, form is the clue to content, and content the clue to form. *Portrait of a Scholar* (page 126) is at first sight nothing but a construction, but the form gradually emerges—a reality that had not possessed existence before and that now becomes something else besides a form, the reflected image of "some remote power." Without the title we would scarcely suspect what is intended in the drawing; only once it has been "baptized" do we feel that hand and spirit, object and subject, converge. "Whenever, as often happens, a picture can be compared to something else, then it is a kind of simile," Klee said in one of his lessons. "And like all similes, pictures may have many meanings. In which case another simile may apply. What speaks in similes is poetic—poetic, not literary. . . . To make a poem is to pick and choose words in such a way that they give rise to a metaphor; then striking images are created."

Klee's humor is a component of his poetic vision. According to Goethe, humor is born when things slip outside the orbit of reason, and reason lets itself be teased by them. Many of Klee's works fall within this definition, but the humor lies more often in the forms than in the themes. There are amusing contrasts even in some of the early drawings, such as the *Two Aunts* (1908; page 53) with its tension between theme and gesture, line and expression. In later works humor gradually involves the pictorial elements themselves. In the drawing of Don Juan (1913; page 61) there is an anecdote to lean on, but not in the *Ghost of an Ancient Hero* (1918; page 72). In *Suis-je belle moi?* (1939; page 155) the tension lies entirely in the contrast between the precise construction and the absurdity of the question. What is the meaning of *Reflective Wanderer* (1931; page 129)? The geometrically exact figuration is in the strongest possible contradiction to the title, but the forms suggest the route being followed, and thus the sense of strained technical effort is gently mocked. Klee's humor did not slacken even in his last year: *Family Quarrel* (1940; page 162) is one of the last examples.

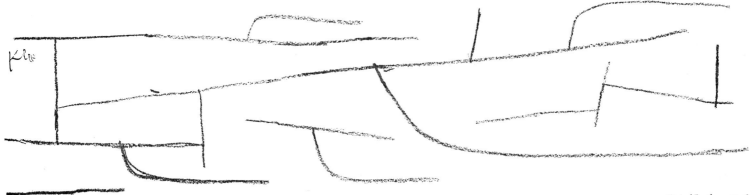

Canal Locks 1938

4 The Drawings

a. Early Works: Bern and Munich

Klee began to draw as a boy, in the margins of his textbooks and in his copybooks, most often treating subjects connected with his classes, but not invariably. His propensity for satire, so strongly marked in the Bern etchings of 1903-5, showed itself early, as did also his conscientious concern for accuracy. He may have been influenced by Jugendstil illustrations in books and magazines, but there is the drawing *My Den* (1896; page 49) in the Biedermeier style, which is totally different. Klee destroyed most of his drawings made at the Munich academy (except for some nude studies). Similarly, almost none of the preliminary drawings for his pessimistic early etchings have been preserved.

In his own catalogue Klee lists only 11 drawings from the period between 1899 and 1904; almost all of them are female nudes. "Sexual helplessness begets monsters of perversion." He lists some portraits and other drawings of men done before 1906, the year he married and moved to Munich. The first listings of landscape drawings appear in 1907, and by 1908 the repertory of the early works is almost complete.

The year 1905 produced *Man with Barrel Organ* (page 51), as well as a pencil drawing with wash of his fiancée, Lily, some etchings, and paintings on glass; this is the first productive year, with 39 items. Belated anatomical studies, poetic satire, and gloomy humor overlap. Klee's line acquires a certain freedom, and now he sets his sights a little higher. "Beauty is not an attribute of the object, but of the pictorial rendering," he notes in his diary, referring to *Man with Barrel Organ*. This figure is more plausible than the erotic nudes, in which he also attempted to represent nonvisible elements, and in which he experimented with a slightly more naturalistic, less classical style than that of the etchings. The pendulum has swung back: the etchings have awakened him to the dangers of ornamentalism. Klee tries to avert it by executing landscape studies. In 1908 in Munich he is still drawing streets and squares, sometimes showing children at play or passers-by. In addition he produces a very different kind of drawing, such as *Two Aunts* (page 53), and *Four Nudes, Mother and Children Apprehensive over Father's Return* (page 52). Both drawings are psychological and "anatomical" improvisations. Klee had by then seen works by Van Gogh and Ensor, which encouraged him to greater freedom, and he deliberately exaggerates his line—in *Two Aunts* to the point of grotesqueness, and in *Four Nudes* with almost baroque rhetoric. The pointed forms of the aunts with their bonnets, and his over-all emphasis on detail lead to an effect of strangeness, which underlines the effort to achieve a style.

After 1908 he produces some naturalistic black-and-white watercolors, on glass and on paper, and after 1909 pen-and-brush drawings in India ink—*Boy in Fur Coat* (page 55) and *Friends Visiting a Sick Girl* (page 54). *Boy in Fur Coat* exists in another, fairly realistic version on the verso of a watercolor in black, *Little Lamp in the Studio* (1909, private collection, U.S.A.) which is not listed in the catalogue. In the grainy ink drawing the figure looks like a piece of old bark, cracked, stringy, fungoid, reminiscent of a parasitic plant; the features with the narrow eyes set wide apart and the long line of the nose has an unfathomable, Mongolian quality. We see that Klee is now thinking about something else besides the model, as he scratches and washes and invents effects that can hardly fail to distract him from the face he is drawing. This very complication stimulates him. The figures of the sick girl and her friends are no less pseudorealistic. To be sure, everything is supplied—faces, poses, proportions, expressions—but if we look more closely, we find that all this is actually a mass of grainy ink spots, within which the features are delicately inscribed. The final effect is a kind of morbid elegance. There is no precedent for this drawing, unless in Post-Impressionist music, such as Debussy's *Pelléas et Mélisande*, which Klee had heard in Munich.

Tidy Path in Woods near Bern (1909; page 57) could be classified as a black-and-white watercolor, but is listed as an India-ink drawing. Klee varies his descriptions of the medium—sometimes he distinguishes between a wash drawing and watercolor with pen, and it is not always clear why. In the last-named drawing he is concerned with problems of tonality and light. He uses white highlights, and achieves effects of black depth "by softly murmured modulations." Furthermore Klee observes that light sets the forms in motion, bends the straight lines, and shapes the intermediate spaces; from these effects he derives stimulation to construction, and guidance in making use of accidents. At the same time he experiments with hairline strokes, and draws sensitive landscapes of the country around Bern and Munich: the quarries of Ostermundigen (1909; page 59), the slopes around the Thunersee, and the suburban villas of *Near Munich* (1910; page 59), repeated as an etching, 1910, 112). The delicate, harmonious arrangement of the lines brings to mind the etchings of Corot, which Klee had admired at an exhibition in Geneva. Klee's line is more deliberate and more rhythmic.

Klee was not satisfied with these drawings. He had to do them, but he thought they were too "optical." He rediscovered himself, as he put it, in the 26 illustrations for Voltaire's *Candide* (1911; page 60). The famous novel fascinated him for years, but his "illustrative style" was not yet perfected. The best of all possible worlds, seen in the shifting mirrors of ridicule, gaiety, and a pessimism bordering on absurdity, was a perfect subject for him. He conveys the absurd note with arabesques of lemurlike figures and spectral horses, elements only touched on superficially in the novel. The words and the pictures are no more related than are the words of Stefan George's poems and Schönberg's music for them, in the songs written about the same period. At all events, the task proved so difficult that Klee tackled it only once more, when he "illustrated" C. Corrinth's *Potsdamer Platz* in 1920. He declined all other offers to illustrate books. He once suggested that perhaps among his many drawings some could be found suitable as illustrations—for instance, for Léon-Paul Fargue's poems.

The term "illustrative style" is perhaps more apt when applied to Klee's drawings of harlequins and grotesque animals (from 1912 on) and to the "anecdotal" drawings from 1913 on, with which Klee had his first commercial success. *Der Sturm* (Berlin) published reproductions of some of these, including *An Angel Hands Over What Is Desired* (1913) and *Suicide on Bridge* (1913); the latter theme will turn up again. But Klee keeps on experimenting, striking out in new directions, and going back to earlier ideas, as in the *Head of a Young Pierrot* (perhaps a portrait of his son Felix, 1912; page 63) and *Street in Latin Quarter* (1912; page 62), both ink drawings with wash, like the *Self-Portrait* and the portrait of *Hannah* of 1910. The combination of line and cloudlike areas produces a very mysterious effect: where the line cuts the area, it runs off to both sides, and line and area are in uneasy balance. Klee now begins to calculate his values as sensitively as Cézanne his spots of color. The *Sketch for Portrait* (self-portrait, 1913; page 65) produces the same formal effects, although the contrasts between light and dark are stronger, and the outlines of the naïve figurations are concealed by black areas.

Klee's anecdotal style, which inaugurates in 1913 a long series of sketches of unusual thematic interest, was considered "naïve" or "infantile" by his contemporaries. But Klee continued to develop this method right on into the Weimar period of the Bauhaus. He was particularly untouched by the criticism of childishness. "Children," he observed, "can do it, too, and there is wisdom in the fact that they can do it." He felt that it was better to go back to the origins than to try to resuscitate a dead tradition. The figures are either painters' manikins, such as are used in art schools, or nudes treated as manikins. *The Last Stage of Don Juan's Infatuation* (1913; page 61) is a riot of passionate movements and lascivious gestures, the forms of which have something of the urgent quality of Mozart's music. Klee must have had in mind Mozart's opera, though he may also have recalled the poems of Byron and Nikolaus Lenau, which he knew. Klee was rarely again to be so vehement and unrestrained as in these drawings made between 1913 and 1915, or as witty and precise in his definition of human figures. The drawings of Kirchner and Kokoschka of 1913 superficially resemble these, but on closer comparison the vast individual differences among these painters becomes unmistakable. Klee's manikins—whether in *Don Juan*, *Warlike Tribe*, or *A Good Joke* (1913; page 4)—precisely because they are as concise as possible, possess all the elements they need in order to be alive and to constitute a picture. There is a stage, there is a plot, and the plot develops. What we have here is a theater that needs no props or sets; the figures and the graphisms are self-sufficient.

The drawings in this style would alone have been enough to assure an artist a permanent place in his epoch; to Klee they represented one possible path among many. Even in 1913 he began to make sketches of an entirely different character. *Flight to the Right, Abstract* (page 170) is a construction like the drawing of 1913, *Linear Construction*. Referring to the latter, Klee noted in his diary: ". . . a real declaration of my love for art. An abstraction from this world—more than a game, and less than a this-worldly collapse. "It does not reflect Kandinsky's influence; Klee had long been aiming at a graphic art which could be defined as "the expressive movement of a hand equipped with a pencil to record it." These were restless times. There was talk about impending war (Kandinsky mentioned this in a letter to the American collector, Arthur

Jerome Eddy), and Klee noted in his diary: "The more terrors this world is full of (as today), the more abstract art becomes; only a happy world gives rise to a this-worldly art." He said that he was leaving the this-worldly region for another world, one that is whole. "Create an art that goes beyond the object, such an art as Hausenstein, in his book on Kairouan, believes to be inescapable." Klee was not sure about the inevitability. He wondered whether he were not himself "turning into the crystalline type."

Drawings such as *Flight to the Right*, so pure in their linear relations, exerted a strong influence on Klee's development. Many drawings of 1913 and 1914, including those containing recollections of the familiar world, are as crystalline in character as *Flight to the Right*. *Song of Lamentation* (1913; page 67) and *Before the Resurrection* (1913), the *Fabulous Island* (1913; page 66), *Jerusalem My Chief Joy* (1914; page 68), and the untitled "vignettelike" drawing of 1915 (page 69) are all building to some level of absolute definition. "Small-scale contrasts linked compositionally, but also large-scale contrasts to oppose order and chaos, for instance, so that the two distinct groups set one beside or above the other, may enter into relationship with each other—the relationship of contrasts, whereby the oppositions on both sides enhance each other. . . . If there were an inner need, the ability would begin to develop" (Diary). Such were the ideas that preoccupied Klee in 1913.

Two Acrobats on a Ladder with a Heart 1918

21

Not all the drawings mentioned above come equally close to the goal. *Song of Lamentation* contains curved figurations, hatchings, and signs. We do not know whether we are supposed to discover fragments of figures or landscapes in this ordered chaos of elements, any more than in the well-known *Garden of Passion* (1913). It is possible that the curving lines of *Lamentation* allude to something recognizable. Thematically clearer are *Fabulous Island* and *Medieval City*, the former drawing with little pyramids and small cubic forms in horizontal arrangement, the latter arranged vertically like a fortification, with structures suggesting old walls with ladders, houses, and bushy sheaves of lines. The "vignettelike" drawing can be interpreted as a landscape or a figurative work; there is a heart-shaped form, and stairs or limbs of the human body; at all events, the horizontal hatchings do not interrupt the climbing, rising rhythm. *Jerusalem My Chief Joy* is a still more daring construction, a paean of three vertical voices which barely touch one another compositionally, so that the expression of rapture is free from any earthly suggestion. Titles such as *Abstract*, *Warlike*, or *Not Quite Heavy Pathos* point in the direction of the still more unrealistic sketches of that period, one of which is *Like a Stage Landscape* (1917; page 70).

As mentioned earlier, the trip to Kairouan marked a turning point in Klee's career. He became a painter—but he did not produce any fewer drawings than before. There were 92 in 1914, and 115 in 1915. The oriental lyricism of the watercolors is matched by the monotonous melodiousness of line (*Sketch from Kairouan*, 1914; page 8). The year 1916 was a lean one: Klee was called to military service, but the lithograph *Destruction and Hope* shows that he continued to work in the "cool" romantic manner. The latter characterizes a great many of the drawings done in the last years in Munich, down to 1920. *Sleep* (1915), *Refined Boor* (1917), and *Constructive Linking of Earth and Heaven* (1918) are drawings without any center of gravity, which defeat the keenest surveyor—metaphors of the universal rather than of the earthly. With them belong *Drawing for Evil Star of Ships* (1917; frontispiece; the watercolor is of 1919), *Drawing with Fermata* (1918; page 73), and *Bird Airplanes* (1918; page 75). In the first of these a number of steamboats and sailboats are grouped around the fish at the center (which is replaced with concentric circles in the watercolor), so that some of them are upside down. No matter how you turn the drawing, the fleet revolves around the center; the black star at the top is the evil star, and no moon of salvation makes its appearance, as it does in many other drawings of the same period. In the watercolor, a Roman cross sets the seal of doom. Cannot there be tragedy without human participants—as, perhaps, in the drawing entitled *Thoughts* of the same year? There is no action of any kind in the *Drawing with Fermata*. Or is there after all? Perhaps broken parallels are enough to suggest it. Here they are quite eloquent, ending as they do in lines that look like trees, branches, flags, and the necks of birds. There is an accent over the *B*, so we must be careful. The *fermata* in music does not merely denote a pause longer than usual, it may also signal the beginning of a brilliant cadenza. The title is not to be taken too literally, but Klee does obtain an effect of surprise, by delaying resolution and placing the star at the upper left as a final chord.

Bird Airplanes with its overlapping rectangles shows structures that are at once birds and flying machines. They look very much like birds dropping to earth or pigeons gliding down. Klee in those years liked to use these birds as metaphors of rise and

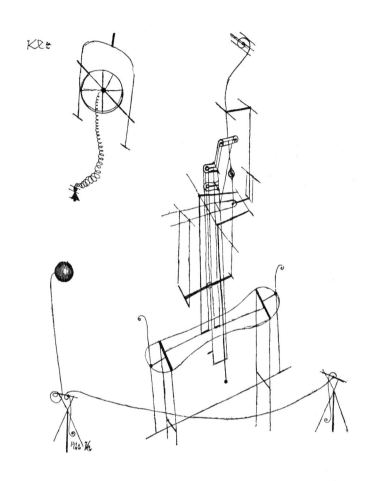

Equipment for Advanced Acrobatics   1922

fall, of gravity and the surmounting of gravity. At the airfield near Augsburg, where he was sent for training, he had a good chance to observe planes, and when he accompanied troop transports he witnessed dogfights in the air and saw planes fall to earth. The arrows suggest an attack, but Klee is less interested in the drama than in the inexorable interlocking arrangement of the rectangles, which alone determines the expression. "We explore forms for the sake of expression and for what we learn thereby about our soul" (Diary, 1917). In his compositions, Klee collects experiences about himself—not about his personal self, but himself as "a neutral creature." *Drawing for "Star Container"* (1921; page 88) continues the series of the Munich years, and like all those drawings is "abstract with recollections." On the complicated radarlike screen there are the letters "St.," which Klee himself interpreted as "star," but which probably stand for something entirely different.

23

A last group of compositional drawings dates from 1920 when Klee was appointed teacher at the Bauhaus. They show straight parallels or bent horizontals, on which "the action" is recorded, like a kind of musical notation. The landscapes with trees, where the tree tops look like notes scored on musical staves, are similar in appearance—*Donkey in Garden*, for instance. The trunks and the tops of the trees (notes and their stems) fill the horizontal bands, and the donkey's legs are incorporated in this pictorial idea. More dramatic is the action in *Composition on Parallel Horizontals* (1920; page 78), in which the staves are crowded with all sorts of lively things. As for *Dance of the Veils* (1920; page 80), we are not sure whether the horizontals are meant as a grid or a flowing robe; the little circle at the center, which looks like a thumbtack on the puppet, unquestionably breaks the epic flow of the lines.

Klee's most successful pictures and drawings of 1920 were illustrative in character—as were *Two Acrobats on a Ladder with a Heart* (1918; page 21), *Ringing for Fish* (1919; page 76), and *They Swallow the Bait*. Klee became better known through these works. When exhibited at the first important exhibition in which he participated (Golt, Munich), they sold quite well. Associations provoked by the pictorial ensemble make it easy for the viewer to see no more than the action, with whatever poetic or humorous overtones it may have, and to look upon the deformations determined by the more essential dimensions of the drawing as a necessary evil. The naïvely outlined fishermen cast their lines beyond the lighthouse, but the fish haven't made up their minds yet. Only the smaller ones, apparently, "swallow the bait." The largest looks like a submarine, the lighthouse looks like a buoy, and the disk of the sun looks like a balloon (the watercolor in the Tate Gallery, London, is somewhat richer). Similarly, in *Ringing for Fish*, the long-nosed fisherman rings the bell, and holds his net ready. In the 1920s fish played an even more prominent part in Klee's production: *Goldfish*, *Fish Magic*, and *Around the Fish* are major paintings of symbolic significance. Here the effect is merely comic. This is certainly not "cool" Romanticism, nor is it "cool" Klee. And who are those peculiar figures climbing a ladder that grows like a neck from a torso, and ends in a heart? Klee invites the viewer to use his own imagination; he does not kill the point of his joke. On the other hand, *Black Magician* (1920; page 81) is anything but gay; the effect of patchiness, of fragmentation—which appears here for the first time—almost arouses anxiety. This magician is unquestionably calling up evil spirits, though they are not triumphant; they are "contributing factors of the creation." The form (a star?) in the upper left corner takes part in all this, much against its will.

Quite apart in the series is *Park on Lake* (1920; page 83), a throwback to the black-and-white watercolor. *Artist Pondering* (page 77), one of the four self-portraits of 1919, is more natural, more "organic," than the other heads of that period. The majority derive from a purely graphic idea, like *Ghost of an Ancient Hero* (1918; page 72), which anticipates the parallel figurations of 1926, but which is based upon earlier studies, such as *Blue-Eyed* (1912). However various Klee's starting points may be, in the last analysis the paths come together. What was unconscious yesterday becomes conscious tomorrow, but at the same time every night's sleep keeps alive the self's primal unawareness.

b. The Bauhaus Period: Weimar and Dessau

In January, 1921, Klee left Munich, only a few weeks after receiving the invitation to teach at the Bauhaus in Weimar. This period of his life is the best known; Klee appeared more often in public than ever before or after. He was in contact with his students and there were always many visitors to the institute. He did not resume his earlier hermitlike existence until late in 1933, when he left Germany. The years at the Bauhaus were happy ones, rich in stimulation and invention. He produced a great deal of work and many of his paintings and drawings done at this time are eloquent of the joy it was to him to experiment in any direction he liked.

From those of 1921 on, Klee's drawings, like his other works, can be arranged in groups, according to the type of pictorial invention embodied in them. All of them suggest recollections of nature; they are images in response to nature, as Goethe would have said. And Klee responds to the world with his whole being.

The variety of his work does not derive from the subjects or themes chosen, for these are merely the outcome, the result. What Klee was interested in was his initial premise. His hand was "the instrument of some distant power." To establish communication with that power, many conditions had to be met, and years of experience accumulated. The latter were fertile to the degree they produced pictorial forms; these forms reflect nature just as much as the artist's hand or mind. We may call such forms "projects" or "schemata." The latter term is sometimes used in this sense in scientific literature.

The schemata of the Bauhaus period are of three kinds: first, those we shall call "peripheral," constituting "the outer circle" of his work, in which we still recognize a starting point in nature; second, the works whose meanings are concealed in an intricate pattern of signs and elements; and third, symbolic works, almost indecipherable in terms of the given pictorial elements, whose meaning is to be found only by retracing the process of creation or by comparing them with other works. Often the pictorial elements themselves provide the answer; they may be "abstract" or they may not. Klee was concerned "less with the question of the existence of the object than with its type."

Concerning the Fate of Two Girls (1921; page 84) is an example of the "peripheral" drawings of the Weimar years. The figures (actresses or ballet dancers) are anything but lifelike taken separately, but taken together they do bring to mind some children's performance, such as the artist may have attended, either at the Bauhaus or in a theater. Klee loved opera, especially enjoying—along with the music—the illogical, improbable dramatic atmosphere. The hem of one girl's skirt and the hairdo of another seem to turn themselves into treble clefs, and the stage itself into a tight rope. The *Village Clown* (1925; page 100) also might be a figure from the theater; the dry-brush technique makes the "clown" appear even more slovenly than he is. This may have been a drawing for his son Felix's marionette theater—Klee drew several sketches for puppets. Or had father and son been to the circus? *Grotesques from the Circus*, executed at about the same time, is in the same manner. Even *Harlequin on Bridge* (1923; page 97) is very theatrical; we can make out both stage and curtains. The harlequin has a long history as one of Klee's motifs, first appearing in *Der Sturm's* book of reproductions as *Suicide on Bridge* (1913). It turns up again in 1923 in a watercolor. The works of this year are full of references to marionettes, opera, magicians. Does the *Portrait of an Expressionist* (1922; page 92) also belong among these? Is this "expressionist" a playwright or an actor? Note that the treble clef appears in this also. As a physiognomical motif, it goes with the *Pathetiker*, showing the figure of an actor, done the same year.

Not quite so obviously theatrical are drawings like *Comedy* (1921; page 85), *Costumed Puppets* (1922; page 91), and the grotesque *Dance You Monster to My Sweet Song* (1922; page 89). If there are theatrical allusions here, they refer to some theater purely of Klee's imagining. *Costumed Puppets* comes closest to suggesting the stage, but apart from the figures' roughly human proportions, all is invention here. These figures are composed of formal ornaments, made up of musical symbols both large and small, together with simple spirals and spirals that wind and unwind more erratically to form coils, tiny wheels, and dots. These elements compose not only the costumes, but the puppets themselves, which function as such because we can see every detail of their construction, and they come to life in pictorial terms. The fact that the figures are

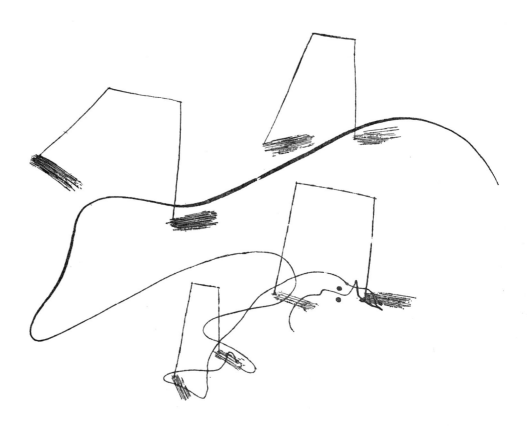

26   *Dreamy 1930*

so plausible seems the result of accident or luck, however, rather than design. Klee himself would have said that such figures are truer than nature, for they do not drag along with them the whole weight of physical and spiritual existence. In *Comedy* (1921; page 85) the over-all effect depends on the grotesqueness of the individual details, while in *Dance You Monster* a hallucinated quality predominates. No one is tempted to make comparisons between this drawing and any other. This extraordinary head, which is set on a stand, is recognizable as a head only because of the eyes. Without them it would be an impersonal apparition. The monstrous is here given a purely pictorial definition, of a kind Klee achieved quite often in works of the Weimar period. The evil apparition is evidently under the control of the tiny figure at the bottom, who manipulates a sort of lyre. The primordial male principle of evil and the primordial female principle of good here tend toward "a state of ethical stability."

Governess (1922; page 90) and *Fashion Picture* (1922; page 93) are specimens of Klee's skill at fixing types, a skill as remarkable in its breadth as the skill he possessed for creating physiognomic patterns. In neither case is the result one of deliberate construction of a mental model: it always emerges spontaneously. When Klee's pen or pencil took one of its "walks" it led him as surely as a sleepwalker to very concise forms suggestive of specific ideas. The corrugated paper forms on the heads of the governess and the child may suggest either marcelled hair or some sort of hat—in any case, they are funny, and the impression of ridiculousness is enhanced by the curve of the shoulder (a fur piece?) and by the S-shaped lines. The other drawing suggests a fashion model, "classical" because of the pseudoantique ornamentation and stupid "cowlike" eyes. No matter what subject Klee evokes—artist, saint, or fashion model—the form is a combination of precise elements, and emerges as a reality truer than life, because it epitomizes many realities.

Weimar, a small town with a glorious past, stimulated Klee's gift for ironical comment. No sphere of life or culture was sacred, once Klee's sense of humor was engaged. Among his drawings of this period are *Astrological Charlatans*, *Aging Venus*, *Message to the Proletariat*, and *South-American Landscape with Two Llamas*. They all reflect Klee's relaxed mood after the strenuous Munich years. His inventions in the line of mechanical apparatus are especially eloquent in this vein. The most delightful single example is the *Twittering Machine* (a drawing for it is entitled *Branch Concert*, 1921); also *Equipment for a Doctor's Office* and *Equipment for Advanced Acrobatics* (1922; page 23) are inspirations of a witty artist, who had his own way of coping with modern technological civilization.

Between the "peripheral" or "outer circle" group and the "inner circle" group of symbolic drawings there falls a group characterized by inventions in graphic technique. Among these are the fur-textured hatchings of *Still Life of Bazaar* (1924; page 95), the spraying process used in *Oriental Girl* (1924; page 99), and the cobweb effects of *Façade* (1924; page 96). As also occurs with musicians, so-called "ornaments" may give rise to a broadening or deepening of the formal canon, and eventually to a new schema. Such inventions were almost never casual ideas or passing events to Klee. He was quick to grasp and exploit them, and to realize their deeper significance.

27

Klee used hatchings in accompaniment with line mainly to depict vegetal processes, as in *Cosmic Flora* (1923) or *Growth with Half Moon* (1924). In these works they serve to indicate three-dimensionality, growth, or change. As always in Klee, these technical inventions are quickly extended to the artistic process itself, and applied to quite other uses, in drawings of a different kind. Examples of this are *Still Life of Bazaar* (1924; page 95), *Village with Sunflowers* (1925; page 103), *Physiognomy of a Dream* (1924; page 94), and *Snake with Prey* (1926; page 107). In each case the hatchings produce different effects in conjunction with the lines. Often they are linked with other elements as well, with results totally unlike those first discovered. When Klee was working on *Still Life of Bazaar*, he stated that he was trying to achieve a differentiation of values in the matter of degree rather than intensity. This elaborate assemblage of faintly familiar forms, of odds and ends of all kinds, makes an intricate pattern of lights and darks, of looseness and tightness, and runs a veritable gamut of the possible effects of contrast. In *Mother of Witches* (1925; page 101) the prickles faintly suggestive of body hair underline the nastiness of the theme. In *Still Life with Artificial Flowers* (1925) flowers are by the same invention transformed into cacti, and in *Snake with Prey* the hatchings provide a disquieting musical accompaniment to animal tragedy.

Physiognomy of a Dream is something else again: here the effect of fragmentation is stronger than that of the hatchings, and the conception borders on the symbolic. In Klee, fragments are "signs which have been directly produced by emotion." They are new, purely psychic realities—pseudorealities. They do not reproduce anything else, but are the result of new modifications and creations. They are transformations that give rise to surprising effects. Klee thus touches upon the problem of rebirth in the work of art, the question of metamorphosis. A conception of the dream as a partial waking state of the brain, itself a source of reality—albeit fragmented—obviously fitted into the pictorial schema of this drawing. At all events, *Physiognomy of a Dream* belongs to the "inner circle" of Klee's works.

How ought we to classify the *drawing for "Occupied Room in Perspective"* (1921; page 87)? At first glance, the perspective looks normal, and this is surprising, for, according to Klee, the system of perspective was never anything but an intellectual auxiliary to art. He held that depth is imaginary, and therefore a mystery. Since to Klee movement was always the normal state of things, the point of view in this drawing, as in others, is not a fixed one, but shifts to right and to left. There are three points of view. Moreover, Klee now moves farther into the room, now farther away from it. This results in a certain distortion; also, the hallway near the center considerably adds to the effect of depth, and lends mystery. Even more mysterious are the figures and heads on one wall and on the floor, drawn, like the arrow and the intersecting slanting lines, two-dimensionally. The room becomes haunted rather than inhabited, and evokes a highly complex state of affairs. Klee's architectonic perspectives in works of later years are all of this kind.

During the years the Bauhaus was at Dessau, drawings and paintings alike move from the periphery closer and closer to the center, to "the heart of creation." Fewer and fewer drawings are easy to understand or interpret. More and more fall inside "the inner circle," and can only be grasped by close study of Klee's artistic development.

28

Close to the peripheral group are some pictures of ports and ships, such as *Nine Boats with the Sun* (1926), *Port of Plit* (1927; page 111), and *Frightened Ships* (1927; page 110). From 1924 on, Klee went on several trips to the Mediterranean region—to Sicily and Elba, to Florence, and in 1927 to Corsica and to the island of Porquerolles (1933; page 142). He loved the sea and the sun, the atmosphere of ports where everything stands out in sharp outline and colors are bright. He once spoke of "the stimulation of history combined with that of nature." Wherever he went, he was conscious of the tension between present and past, landscape and culture.

The ships in his drawings they are sometimes geometrically formed and tidily arranged, sometimes sketched very freely and grouped at random. Occasionally, relations between them are controlled dynamically by alternation of heavy lines with lighter ones, so that their position in space, their movements, their relative speeds may be deduced. But where did Klee ever set eyes on the *Dutch Cathedral* he drew (1927; page 113)? Perhaps on troop transports while he was in the army, for he traveled as far as Cambrai and Saint-Quentin. Just a few lines traced with a reed pen suffice to suggest a medieval cathedral in Holland. *Houses in Flames* (1929; page 118) conveys a fugitive impression, set down on the spot. It is not the only drawing in this "open" manner, however. *Sun and Rain* (1929) is of the same type, but more austere and abstract.

Nomad Prince (1929; page 123) and *Preaching to Animals in the Desert* (1929; page 122) are almost narrative in character, probably involving recollections of the artist's trip to Egypt in 1928-29, where he was reminded of Tunis and Kairouan. In *Nomad Prince* appears that "silvery moon" which Klee said he would never forget. The cattle are very "Tunisian" in the first drawing, while the preacher in the second drawing has a "Cubist" head, and a body constructed of intersecting lines—one of the "schemata" of the period.

More intense and bold in expression are some drawings made up of fragmented forms: *Would Should* (1927; page 114), *What a Mess You've Made!* (1927; page 117), and *Losing Control* (1927; page 116). It was the poet in Klee that led him to keep coming back to anecdotal themes, although even here he was always guided by graphic inventions. "What a mess you've made, you really have," he wrote in the drawing. "You should be ashamed of yourselves! Shame on you!" An arrow points to the event depicted—some scene of domestic disorder involving tiny figures. Nearly all of the latter are split up, fragmented; this means they are only half real, half logical. Among the hatchings we find a head, a head with legs, a body without a head, and scattered limbs of all kinds, the total effect an unpleasant one of decomposition. A large number of the other drawings of 1927 show fragmented bodies, with hatchings growing out of their parts like moss. For all their ugliness, these drawings are not devoid of humor. Klee had previously made experiments along this line in Weimar: *Scene from the Drama of a Stable Master* (1923), for example, in curly lines. There is another example of narrative technique in *Demonism* (1925). Now he builds on the sum total of his previous experiments and arrives at desperate glimpses of what goes on behind the surface of appearances, as in *What a Mess You've Made!* and *Would Should*, the most abstruse of these drawings. Everything has fallen apart; furry antennae wave aimlessly in space. Because of the disjunction, the figures also move limply in time. As in music, the tension lies between the notes. Was this last-named drawing meant to be comic or tragic? "Would" the figure go or "should" it? The high-heeled shoes evoke an *opera buffa*, but there is something very unfunny about the seated or reclining figure on the right, and the lighted candle provides a spectral touch. These scenes are haunted; another such drawing is *Woo, Brawl, Kill* (1927). They tell a continous story, as did the drawings for *Candide*—"the best of all possible worlds" in a new version, with captions by Klee.

It hardly comes as a surprise that the somewhat geometric drawing *Ship on Course* (below), *Constructive Play* (page 1), and *Excitement Before Trip* (page 14) were made the same year as those just discussed. They are true opposites, and what Klee did was to expose the mystery that lies hidden in the constructive, and the schema that is concealed in the obvious. In *Ship on Course* we might be looking at a difficult navigational problem solved pictorially with two arcs and two dynamic accents. Probably Klee had some knowledge of the stars and of how their positions are determined in navigation. Moreover, his interest in the stars was always astronomical, not astrological. Although the drawing consists of very few lines, it is rich in meaning. Here, as in *Excitement Before Trip*, Klee's approach is pedagogic: his starting point was theory, understood as "an expedient of clarification." The latter drawing consists of nervous accents, as he put it, in explaining lines that become flesh, of linear bodies that suddenly expand. As it "progresses," linear construction gradually disappears as such, to become an integral part of the structural design. This sounds very abstruse, but it was one of Klee's most fundamental points in his classes on art. Once the construction is complete, viewers take their own different lines of approach to

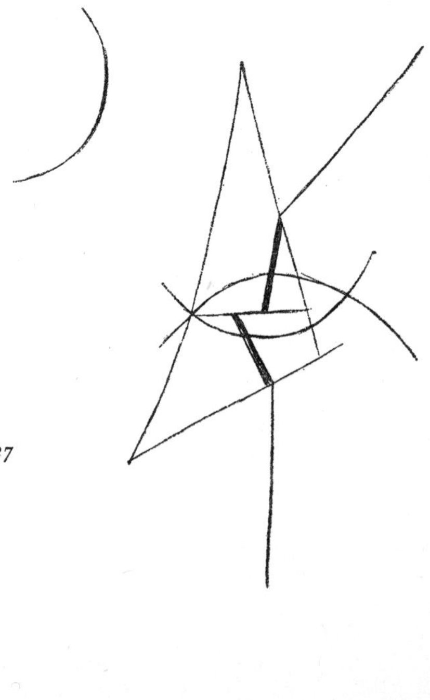

Ship on Course   1927

what a picture may mean: a dot in a hexagon may look like an eye in a head; forms may become a ship or limbs that may be running somewhere. Klee was a mathematician in Novalis' sense, when he called mathematics the highest form of poetry.

More frequently, the geometric elements are simpler. *Reflective Wanderer* (1931; page 129), like the better-known *Family Going for a Walk* (1930), is an ensemble of geometric planes. This drawing, too, is based on Klee's theory of art; in the list of his works Klee wrote next to the title: "Double projection along vertical axis," and this is directly followed in the list by *Model (Disk Fragments), Distorting Mirrors, Triangles in Pairs on Different Levels.* These drawings, it is clear, do not always evoke associations; often the geometric designs serve to illustrate certain functions and give no clue as to the creative method applied.

However, solving mathematical problems may have been for Klee an important bond with reality, and the same may be even truer of such architectonic constructions as *City Waterfront I* (1929; page 124) and *Further Study in Three Dimensions* (1930; page 125). In Dessau, Klee made many drawings of city scenes. *City with Watchtowers* (1929) is a recollection of San Gimignano, and *Santa A in B* (1929) evokes another of the Italian cities he visited. Here he was concerned with the problem of dimensions and the contrast of "endotopic" with "exotopic." "What is treated on the picture surface as exotopic has a tendency to stand out, while endotopic elements recede. A work is three-dimensional when what is inside and what is outside can be clearly distinguished." These are his own words, but more comes into these drawings involving architec-

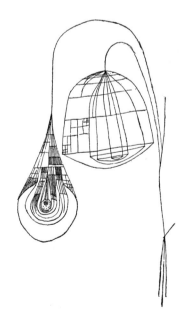

Two Blossoms 1927

31

ture. As early as 1901, during a visit to Italy, he had reflected at length about architecture and the problem of materiality in relation to it. Klee was a rebel where the material was concerned, and he excluded it from his discussion of the three dimensions. All this comes into an understanding of these drawings, which at first glance seem no more than travel sketches. In *Further Study in Three Dimensions*, the variations in perspective are more complicated; in addition there is the transparency of matter in space, which relates this drawing to those showing flying bodies or folding boxes—*Sailing City* and *Braced Planes* (1930). This architectural and mathematical study may be said "to fly"— i. e., there is movement and dynamism as well as matter transparent in space. Klee was convinced that ideas of this kind arise solely out of seeing things as they really are. He believed that most people see space as they were taught to see it, and for this reason are unaware of the problems involved in three-dimensional seeing. Does *Enforced Outcome* (1934; page 145) belong to this group? Elements of both space and movement are present, but there is also an arrow that tries vainly to break out of a labyrinth of intersecting straight lines (another schema). Arrows always signify tragedy—"the tragedy of having to become movement and not to be." Unlike the technical and formal inventions of the Weimar years, the graphic schemata executed in Dessau reach down more deeply into the unconscious and evoke modes of thinking rather than narrative actions. In them, inventive instinct is closely linked with reflection. Among these works are the drawings composed of parallel lines—"parallel figurations"— such as *View of a Mountain Shrine* (1926; page 105); the filigreed traceries of the *Beride* series, e. g., *The Great Dome* (1927; page 10); the drawings in which line has a musical character, e. g., *Under the Angel's Wing on a Steep Path* (1931; page 131); and nonfigurative drawings using discontinous line, e. g., *Dreamy* (1930; page 26). For months at a time Klee did nothing but draw, working "with barbaric savagery," and there were days when he produced whole series of drawings.

Unlike the drawings just mentioned, which belong to the "inner circle" of Klee's work, others of the same period are easy to interpret. Among such, for instance, are *Exit* (page 139), *What a Proposal!* (page 141), *A Poet Pregnant* (page 140), and its predecessor, *Hamlet Maybe?* (page 133). All of these involve experiment, for we can recognize only a lady of fashion wearing a hat with feathers, a shawl, and a filmy gown, or a poet of decidedly comic features. The title of the visionary drawing *Hamlet Maybe?* asks the viewer to participate in the artist's invention—much as Goethe occasionally would ask a friend to tell him what the "fairy tale" he had just written was really about. Klee's profound understanding of people comes out in all these drawings. Not only familiar facial types, but all conceivable physiognomic possibilities were stored in his imagination, "physiognomic" being taken to include both features and expressive movement. Klee is fascinated by Hamlet as an antithesis to Faust; in other drawings he is fascinated with the gently humorous contrast between the substantiality of the figure and the relative simplicity of the idea expressed.

There is a group of drawings, each of which involves graphic inventions never subsequently followed up. This group includes: *Windmill Flowers* (1926; page 109), one work in the series of *Dynamoradiolaria* all done that year; *Lap Dog I* (1932; page 134) with its poodle effects of line; *Old Maid* (1931; page 127), seemingly a tangled unraveling of a single line; *Two*

Blossoms (1927; page 31), which exploits an almost microscopic thinness of line; and *Big Circus* (1928; page 121), in which the gradation in density of line develops an idea implicit in *Excitement Before Trip* (1927; page 14). All these inventions might be called "ephemeral," not to suggest that the drawings are in any way inferior, but to denote the fact that they did not lead the artist any further toward symbolism.

By contrast, the "parallel figurations" and the drawings mentioned earlier, involving new uses of both continuous and discontinuous line—all done during the Dessau years—belong to the "inner circle." Here the pictorial form conceals the actual meaning. This is esoteric art; the picture is conceived of as a code, as an interpretation of the world through symbols, the symbol being understood as "a thing that is not a thing, yet is a thing, an image condensed in the mirror of the spirit and yet identical with the object." (The words are Goethe's, from his essay on Philostratus.) The pictorial treatment is rigorous here, too, although the part of unconscious creativity is greater than usual.

The drawings exploiting parallel lines—Klee called them "radiating parallels"—may be related to the principle of imitation in musical composition. Groups of parallel straight lines and curves determine the formal ensemble by the way they are arranged and knit together. The groups constitute flat forms suggestive of architectural or landscape forms, and the curves delineate figures.

View of a Mountain Shrine (1926; page 105), *Garden for Orpheus*, and *Adrasteopolis* (1926) are among the major works in this series, almost all of which are of a classical Greek character. We are reminded of Greek temples, and yet we know that the latter could not have served as the artist's starting point; this was provided, rather, by the Greek tragedies Klee was so fond of. It may have been while working out these parallel figurations, both horizontal and vertical, that he stumbled upon the principle of stairs, steps, columns, and gateways. Where the lines overlap or interlock, he may have discovered the principle of plants. In the end his view of Greece was that it serves as a kind of archetype, capable of suggesting devices for getting us out of our difficulties, showing us how to improve the "unsatisfactory spots." Archetypes do have a generative power and are related to symbols. Klee's notion of Greece was not historical; it reappears time and again at various places, according to the needs of meaning or technique. This was what he referred to when he spoke of "the alliance between our conceptions of the world and purely artistic exercises." One might also say that the style of the graphic elements in these parallel figurations incorporates the Greek style, giving rise, in combination with the *eidos* of the country, to a mountain shrine or an Orphic garden.

In his figurative drawings Klee treats the schema somewhat more freely. Curving or spiraling parallels may result in other themes, and suggest other pictorial elements as the work progresses. In *Bite on the Shoulder* (1926; page 108), along with other forms, he uses the S-shaped form; in *Long Hair and Soulful* (1929; page 128), it is the spiral. Every such schema seems to break down in the course of the work, and Klee has done nothing to arrest this process. As soon as one problem is solved, he starts immediately on the next—and it may be the precise opposite of the last or a development from it.

The recurrent strip-forms, both distinct and interrelated, in the drawings of 1926 are unquestionably survivals of the imitative style. But Klee never entirely abandoned a design. He might go back to it later, or might jump ahead of himself. *Creator* (1930) is based on curving parallels, and *Classical Ruins* (1933) is one of the last of this group. The fact that Klee, eight years after inventing the schema, still uses the word "classical" in the title further suggests that these schemata always evoked for him the spirit of the Greek tragedies.

Whether or to what extent the continuous line drawings may be connected with the parallel figurations is hard to say. What they would seem to have in common is emphasis upon rhythm, fugal arrangement, polyphonic effects. *Gathering Snowstorm* (1927; page 119), however, emphasizes the vertical organization as forward movement in time more clearly than do the classical drawings. In the continuous line drawings, movement in space becomes identical with movement in time.

Closely related are drawings where the line is not exactly continuous. In them occur isolated lines, intersecting lines, and lines that swerve to avoid other lines. The best description of some is that the line is staccato (*Arise*, 1933) or *con anima* (*Laced into a Group*, 1930). Contemporary with these drawings are those of completely discontinuous lines, utilized with great sensitivity, as, for instance, in *Dreamy* (1930; page 26) and *Diagram of the Redemption* (1934; page 44). Linear forms need time, Klee said, and the more time, the farther they extend in space. When they intersect, they give rise to imaginary space, but space is also a temporal concept. Example: *Little Fool in Trance* (1927; page 115), which Klee drew in a single impulse, almost without lifting his pen from the paper. Like the *Allegorical Figurine* (1927), this curious little jester is also, as Klee described it to his students, "an example of movements superimposed upon each other, each of which is conceived of as momentary." We observe the fool and his movements simultaneously from the front and from above; we are made aware both of the figure's self-absorption and of how he is entertaining us. Klee's aim of "simultaneity in many dimensions" is realized here. *Under the Angel's Wing on a Steep Path* (1931; page 131) also achieves simultaneity, the figure under the angel's wing being incorporated in the line that forms the angel. The same schema is less rigorously expressed in *Successful Adventure* (1931; page 37). Discontinuous lines of the pen, the thickening of certain lines, and other variations of emphasis within the drawing areas produce an effect of looseness. There are really two planes, the one in front being fragmented and disquieting, while the other recedes, serving as both link and counterbalance.

Dream and *Disgrace*, both made in 1933, are high points among the discontinuous line drawings. They are ideograms, signs denoting imponderable unconscious states, such as could be experienced, perhaps, only by someone for whom rhythm has at once musical and artistic significance. The melodic possibilities of line assert themselves against all interference in these works, as also against angular obstacles in *Erasing Spirits*. In *Laced into a Group*, the draftsman is so much at one with his idiom that we have the illusion that the group has created itself. During his last years, Klee produced many such works.

Experiment for Antigone (1933; page 138) comes close to the ideogrammic drawings, and is almost impossible to interpret. It must reflect Klee's emotions after he read the famous play in 1932 in "a state of feverish excitement." He was deeply moved by the tragedy of Oedipus' daughter, whom Creon ordered to be buried alive. The lines begin hopefully, expand and contract again, and break off. The dark spots seem to recede—these are emotional gestures of the artist's hand, seeking to transpose literature in line. This is the only known instance of an abstract drawing by Klee based on Greek tragedy. His drawing for Aeschylus' *Suppliants* (1932; page 130), the play about the persecuted daughters of Danaus, is a parody of an actress, and *Before the Temple* (1932; page 132) could be the sketch of a temple in Sicily. Klee was interested in Greek relics, and on his trip there made a pilgrimage to the village of Gela, to commune with the spirit of Aeschylus, who died there.

Similarly ideogrammic are the brush drawings *Between Autumn and Winter* (1932; page 136) and *Frost* (1932; page 137). In the former, Klee has invented fuzzy clusters of lines that seem meant to provide protection against the cold. Klee often explored areas of sensibility intermediate between a given situation and human reactions to it. *Before the Snow* is another example, which utilizes another schema. *Frost* is yet another, totally different drawing, involving elements of landscape, both vegetation and buildings. The wobbly lines of this drawing teem with allusions to cold weather; the whites are very white, and the black dots and scrawls are like snowflakes.

Recently there has been some discussion of *Portrait of a Scholar* (1930; page 126), which is related to the *Plan for a Castle* of the same year. It is a brush drawing which embodies some purely technical ideas: Klee laid stencils on the paper and worked on the areas left uncovered, repeating this process several times. Here again we are in an "intermediate realm," which is both exact and imaginary. Only when he had completed the work did the artist decide what it suggests. Klee made several "portraits of scholars," but none is as purely a creation *ex nihilo* as this one. The result of his technical operations certainly admits of this particular identification.

Toys 1927   35

c. The Last Years in Bern

By the end of 1933, Klee found himself back in Bern, after thirteen years of work and teaching in Germany. He was to live six more years. He fell ill in 1935 and produced almost nothing in 1936. But toward the end he compensated for his declining physical powers by superabundant intellectual and artistic activity. One of his most productive years was 1939.

His conceptions did not change perceptibly in Bern, at least not at the outset. He worked on, and not until 1937 can we speak of a new period, his last. The first sign of this was a fresh burst of graphic invention—as with the earlier periods— and its last expressions were symbols of transience and the ineffable.

Klee looked back over his life's work and, as often happens in the last years of an artist's life, occasionally took up earlier ideas again. In 1934 he made a drawing echoing his *a-2 Demon* of 1926, and he once more addressed himself to the problem of lighting (*Light Penetrates into the Room*, 1935). He treated several anecdotal subjects (*Beach Resort with Patients*, 1938) and Porquerolles landscapes (*Estate on the Kistler Road*, 1935), and further exploited the schemata of parallel figurations (*Eastern Classic Coast*, 1936) and intersecting curved lines (*Silly*, 1935). There are also physiognomic studies and explorations of intermediate stages (*Stay? Hardly!*, 1938), ideograms and diagrams (*A Storm Coming?*, *Near-by*, 1934), abstract musical themes (*Light Roll of Kettledrum*, 1938), and even the calligraphic signs of the Munich period (*Beginning of a Poem*, 1938). He returned in a sense to everything he had done earlier, but he never repeated himself—not even in the drawings where old schemata are clearly recognizable. For instance, in *Eastern Classic Coast* the intervals between the parallel lines are larger and very different from what they were before, and in *Beach Resort*, while the patients are drawn in the old manner, they are now set among abstract suggestions of landscape. *Light Roll of Kettledrum* is an ethereal cobweb of curves and straight lines. When Klee repeats—and this is also true of his teaching—it is with variations and metamorphoses. And throughout this last period, too, he made drawings that led him on into hitherto unexplored regions.

Symbiosis (1934; page 143) evokes both vegetation and human features. The lines are like wires, and the drawing almost sways in the breeze, like a Calder mobile. Art, to Klee, was as many-sided an activity as nature itself. *Wavy Leaf* (page 42) dates from 1934, the year of the diagrams; it consists of interlocking hook-shaped lines, like *Organ Mountains* of the same year. *Water Route* (1937) anticipates the design of *Canal Locks* (1938; page 17) with its flowing movements, inhibitions, and rhythms.

The first of the drawings done in heavy black brush strokes dates from 1937. The color used in these is pasty and uncompromising, but this is not to say that they are insensitive or that the medium serves only to render harsh conceptions. It would also be wrong to presume that, since Klee was to die in 1940, he lived and worked constantly in the shadow of imminent death, with feelings of hopelessness. Death did not frighten Klee; to him, it spelled the ultimate metamorphosis. Nor did the pace of his inventiveness slow down. Right up to the end, Klee continued to advance. *Little Runaway* (1937;

page 146) is an example of his humor at its most cheerful. The "runaway" was the son of friends, and his escapade worried them. Klee's feelings are reflected in the agitation of the brush strokes. Perhaps he would have wished the drawing to be different—but with Klee, who could predict results in advance? The signs came of themselves and formed a sort of obstacle course. When the little runaway made his appearance, the meaning of the drawing was supplied. Another such drawing is *Oh Dear!* (1937; page 147). Next to *X-chen*, made the same year, this is one of the most affectionate and

Successful Adventure 1931

appealing of his drawings; for all its sadness it is closer to humor than to tragedy. Humor will make its appearance even in the Requiem series that were among Klee's very last works. *They All Run After!* (1940; page 167) is one of the last drawings, and reveals an aspect of Klee's personality that endeared him to many. People, animals, trees—everything is running after the Pied Piper, whom we see from the front and from the side simultaneously, and who is pointing to the exclamation mark.

Family Quarrel (1940; page 162), on the other hand, is a tragicomic footnote on domesticity, while the lady in *Suis-je belle moi?* (1939; page 155) expresses a more malicious observation, which, it is pleasant to note, Klee still had at his disposal. In the latter drawing there is nothing to remind us of nature. Nothing is genuine: the eyes are little wheels, the hair a few doodles, the big hands are shrubs. Every feature is false, yet there can be no question of caricature. For Klee this figure was "a specimen," whose counterpart in real life he had once observed, as any natural phenomenon is observed—say, some exotic bird. Now, during one of the "walks" taken by Klee's pencil, she has turned up in this guise. The drawing with the strange title, *A Nest, Its Coat-of-Arms, Its Future* (1938; page 150), shows a village with a gigantic armorial crest—somehow phony—while over it tower mountains of vanity. It may well be a monument to some pretentious acquaintance whom Klee has provided with a spurious coat of arms. *Animal for a Coat-of-Arms* shows that Klee knew what a real coat of arms was.

Man's fate in this world and in the other is Klee's primary concern in his last years. Although he still draws rocks, trees, animals, and ships, they are treated as individuals rather than as elements of a larger whole. In general they hark back to such drawings as *Heroine* or *Shoulder Birth*. Klee is still interested in the natural process of growth, but now he goes beyond the stage of rendering it by showing us the earth, germinating seeds, etc.—physiological and formal functions, as it were—in transverse and longitudinal section. *Stirrings of Growth* (1938; page 148) and *Vegetation* (1938; page 151) are both brush drawings. The former uses hieroglyphics like those in the later "script" pictures to suggest the tree and its budding branches. The latter might be a forcing bed for young plants in a greenhouse. The forms seem to be sprouting and cover the entire page. "With abstraction reality is bolstered. It makes a bridge to the actual experience of reality." Klee's aim is to track down creation to its source, so as to reveal it in all its functions.

When we spell out the ciphers of nature, it is to rediscover how our own nature is reflected in it. The letters of the alphabet are just such ciphers. *Alphabet II* (1938; page 149) is a brush drawing on a piece of newspaper (Klee also made paintings on newspaper). Here, as elsewhere, he takes advantage of the printed page, which supplies a maximal contrast with his own letters. To such pictures he occasionally gave the name of "poems." "Everything originates from these few signs," Klee said one day, overwhelmed by their expressive force; the letters of the alphabet were for him alive and full of symbolism.

Shortly before his death Klee made a drawing he called *Requiem*. There are angels, ferrymen, and the figure of death.

Another is titled *Ecce* (1940). "Naturally, it is not sheer accident that I am in the tragic vein, so many drawings point in that direction and say, 'The time has come,'" he wrote in a letter early in 1940. In this last period his aim increasingly is to clarify existence and to invoke the absolute. Angels are nothing new in Klee's work. In 1913 there was *Angel Handing Over What is Desired*; in 1920, *Angelus novus*; and in 1931 Klee drew a great many of these enigmatic creatures, with intersecting continuous lines. Now, in 1939, he produced 28, and in 1940, four more. These angels are different from Rilke's angels in the *Duino Elegies*. Klee's are not "the spoilt children of creation." Their habitat is where life and death meet—a region somewhat closer to the invisible than to higher reality. Klee's angels are figures of transition: at the angelic level, the concept of Genesis, of Becoming, and Self-metamorphosis becomes eschatological (*Rock of Angels, Hopeful Angel, Angel's Crisis I*, 1939; pages 157, 159, 161). These drawings are made with pencil in very simple outlines. The line is flexible and avoids expressionistic effects, which would be unsuitable for dealing with the ineffable. In these drawings Klee is as profound and concise as Goethe in the concluding lines of *Faust, Part II*.

Related to the Angels are the series of the Eidola (the archetypes) and the Passion. Among the Eidola are *Former General, Former Opera Buffa Singer, Knaueros Former Kettledrummer*, and *Former Pianist* (1940; page 160). These are ciphers of great exactness, based upon recollection and reflection. For instance, Knauer was the name of a kettledrummer in the Dresden State Orchestra, to whose concerts Klee went when he was in Dresden. He was a genius, Klee said, and this was a term he used sparingly. *Former Pianist* is probably another tribute to an individual, perhaps to Erdmann, who was repeatedly invited to perform at the Bauhaus, or to Serkin, whom Klee met through Adolf Busch and whom he also admired. All personal references have been eliminated, and what remains is the idea alone, directly sketched with unerring sureness in a pictoral schema.

The Passion series includes *Oarsman, Man in the Fifth Row*, and *Dürer's Mother, Too* (1940; page 165), a portrait as poignant as the drawing Dürer made shortly before his mother's death. Did Klee have her in mind or did he also think of Goethe's "Mothers"? The drawing contains no reference to Klee's own mother, long since dead; if it resembles anyone, it resembles Klee's wife, though this is rather hard to specify. *Torch Bearer* (1940; page 163) and *Baptismal Font* (1940; page 164) were executed at about the same time as the drawings for the Passion; they too fall among the Eidola, particularly *Baptismal Font*, though they are not classified as such. The last-named is a final tribute to Italy, one of the places where Klee's imagined "angels" like to live.

One evening while he was working on a drawing Klee said he had the feeling that he was beating a drum. *Drummer's Energies* (1940) and *Injured* (1940; page 168) really are drum beats, impromptu signs, indecipherable as symbols, and yet identical with the subject in each case. Klee's last artistic legacy is thus a simple, direct response to the few calls he could still hear coming from this world and other worlds.

5 Technique

For Klee, there was no such thing as "technique" in a general sense; there was only a technique for each particular case. He used to say that technique is a refined means of expression; it is not something outside the province of the spirit; on the contrary, it presupposes a high degree of delicate sensibility. "Everything must be accounted for down to the last detail."

His studio looked like an alchemist's kitchen. He liked to experiment, and often noted down his procedures, so as to be able to test them later. By its very nature, drawing affords less occasion for experiments than other mediums; nevertheless, Klee's drawing technique is extraordinarily varied. Each time he felt the urge to draw, Klee knew very well whether to choose the pencil, the pen, charcoal, the brush, or more complicated processes. His precreative state of mind seldom misled him as to the means.

In most cases he felt a desire to draw in the evening, after the day's work. He drew with the left hand, or with both hands equally. He was born left-handed, but he had trained himself to use his right hand as well. "Practice, practice," he used to say to his students. "The more skillful your stroke, the more sensitive the results." Training was an integral part of the artist's activity. Although Klee was rarely dissatisfied with a work, he constantly reached higher. He was not concerned with the goal, but only with new ways; the goal would be reached of itself, he knew. He devoted all his energy and intensity to the process of work; he did not calculate the total effect in advance.

Klee did not like to be watched when he painted; but when he drew, this disturbed him little, and it even happened that he drew while his wife was reading to him. His hand ran over the page as though of its own accord, and he listened only when he felt like it. When he wanted, he could cut himself off so completely from the outside world that he saw and heard nothing, and yet was pleasantly stimulated by the presence of another person.

Klee knew all about the different sorts of paper, but until his Bauhaus period he contented himself with ordinary varieties. In Weimar he became more exacting, but without confining himself to specific types. Until 1934 his catalogue does not specify kinds of paper; only from 1935 on does he describe each item: scrap paper, letter paper, graph paper, Ingres, Fabriano, Japan paper, rag paper, wrapping paper, newsprint, Zanders, jute. As late as 1939 he often used scrap paper and letter paper, and occasionally Japan. It is not always clear why he chooses better or poorer sorts of paper. The Passion series, including *Dürer's Mother, Too* (1940), is on Japan paper, while the Eidola series (1940) is on scrap paper.

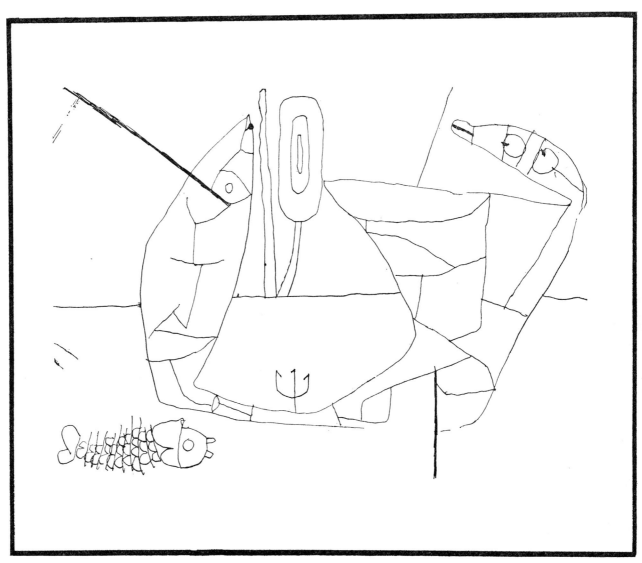

Through Poseidon   1940

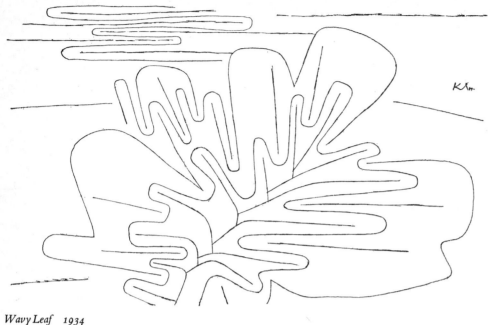

Wavy Leaf 1934

As for his choice of tools, in the early years the pencil predominates, and from 1908 on, the pen (the *Candide* drawings of 1911-12 are pen drawings), which was to remain his favorite instrument. From 1925 on, he used the brush; from 1927 on, the reed pen. Of the 209 drawings of 1927 only four are done in pencil, nine in chalk, seven in chalk and pen; six are tracings, four transfers from greasy paper, the rest are pen or reed drawings. In the late 1920s Klee occasionally used grease crayons and charcoal; in 1931 he used the drawing pen for the mathematical drawings. In 1932 he also used a heavy pencil, which is broader and more suitable for modulating the line. In 1933 he went back to the brush; from 1937 on, he used the brush mostly with paste color; in 1939 and 1940 the pencil predominates again. Furthermore, Klee was familiar with the rubbing process, but used it rarely, mostly in chalk or charcoal drawings (*Further Study in Three Dimensions*, 1930).

He used carbon-paper tracings to repeat a drawing, and also because the line in tracings is more indirect and more lively (*Artist Pondering*, 1919). Since these tracings seemed to him too commercial, he prepared his tracings by covering a page with black oil paint, letting it dry a little, and then pricking the drawing with the needle, so that the resulting line was very diversified. Klee achieves a similar effect by lightly moistening the page or rubbing a little India ink on it, and then working with the pen on the moistened ground (*Street in Latin Quarter*, 1912). When he thinks it necessary he also adds wash to a drawing after it is completed, or adds a few colored accents, as in *Drawing for Evil Star of Ships* (1917). He also used this process in the lithograph *Destruction and Hope* (1916). This concludes the list of his chief techniques.

42

His indications of technical details in the catalogue are, as all his indications, exact but not always clear. In the case of wash drawings, brush drawings, and those with black paste or oil color, the classification varies at times. For reasons that cannot be discerned, he calls some of them "drawings" and others of the same kind "color sketches," where the word "color" may simply mean that the drawing is like a gouache. Actually, these drawings are monochrome (black and white). The same is true of the black-and-white watercolors. Klee does not distinguish between monochrome and polychrome drawings until 1934. Previously he distinguished between drawings and watercolors and, from 1931 on, between drawings and color sketches.

Reproduced in this book are drawings done with thin or broad pencil, pen, reed pen, brush with or without pen, charcoal, grease crayons, red chalk, as well as wash drawings, transfers, tracings or drawings on oil paint, and one charcoal rubbing. In addition there are pen drawings done on wet ground, pen-and-wash-drawings, brush drawings with paste colors, and brush drawings with stencil.

In nearly every case the choice of medium is impressively apt. The meticulous drawings he made as a high-school student required the pen; the nudes and the sketchy *Man with Barrel Organ* (1905), the pencil; *Friends Visiting a Sick Girl* (1909), the combination of India-ink spots and pen, which gives precision and atmosphere. For the biting irony of the *Candide* series (1911-12) with its ghostlike figures, the pen is the only possible instrument, as it is for the sensitive Post-Impressionist landscapes he drew in Munich. Among the many pen drawings of the war years, we find one pencil drawing, *Like a Stage Landscape* (1917); the softer medium is here as appropriate as the harder pen in the exact *Drawing with Fermata* (1918). Klee sometimes experimentally employed several techniques in a single drawing. *Street in Latin Quarter* (1912) is an example of a successful combination of very different techniques. The pen line blends with the ground, and the wash adds an Impressionist quality; the total effect was unquestionably intended and well calculated.

One of the most fantastic technical inventions is the traced-design process, particularly in the so-called oil drawings. Klee aimed at a differentiated line that did full justice to the richness of his variegated techniques, a line that retained its spontaneity and identity and at the same time was susceptible of incorporating accidents, variations of intensity, interruptions, vibrations. Spots made involuntarily by the pressure of the hand on the paper may have come as a surprise to Klee, but once they were there he made the most of them. The oil drawings of the Weimar and Dessau years, like the watercolors, into which Klee traced designs, teem with such accidents and sudden ideas (*Concerning the Fate of Two Girls*, 1921; *Harlequin on Bridge*, 1923).

The importance Klee attached to the accord between technique and subject can well be seen from the following selection of pencil drawings: *Like a Stage Landscape* (1917) is a scene halfway between landscape and theater; *Ghost of an Ancient Hero* (1918) has a rather spectral quality; *Composition on Parallel Horizontals* (1920), with the donkey on the staves, is a crossbreed of a landscape with trees and a musical score; *Black Magician* (1920) takes us to the realm of the unconscious;

Diagram of the Redemption 1934

Physiognomy of a Dream (1924), to that of memory; and *Windmill Flowers* (1926) evokes the metamorphic and transitory forms of nature. Only in *Governess* (1922) could the same effect have been achieved with pen instead of pencil. The fact that *Exit* (1933), *What a Proposal!* (1933), and the later *Scene of Comical Riders* (1935) are heavy-pencil drawings is not surprising: Klee could not have rendered the almost physical presence of the figures and their comicalness by means of any other instrument. Greasy chalk is as appropriate for the treatment of the subjects of desert, nomads, and herds in *Nomad Prince* and *Preaching to Animals in the Desert* (1929) as the reed pen is for *Frightened Ships* and *Port of Plit* (1927). On the other hand, Klee also used the reed pen in *Reflective Wanderer* (1931), where it outlines the geometry of the figures a little more expressively than the pen could have done.

From 1933 on, the number of brush drawings increases steadily. The brush is more effective than the pencil or pen when the purpose is to record an atmospheric metaphor (e.g., *Between Autumn and Winter*, 1932) or to render the vicissitudes of fate with dynamic thickenings and interruptions *(Experiment for Antigone, 1933)*. In *Oh Dear!* (1937) and *Child and Phantom* (1938) the brush produces the rich effects of a gouache or oil painting, while preserving at the same time the ideal quality inherent in the graphic medium by being confined to black and white.

In *With the Angels* (1939), the Eidola series (1940), and the Passion series (1940) Klee goes back to the pencil or heavy pencil. To evoke the ultimate, "the absolute mystery" of the Beyond, the simplest medium is the most effective. Significantly, the diagrams, too (*Laced into a Group*, 1933; and *Diagram of the Redemption*, 1934), are pencil drawings; here, too, we deal with otherworldly messages and secret codes.

Nothing was unimportant for Klee. Even technique had to be "accounted for down to the last detail." Where he left anything to chance, the chance became a springboard for new discoveries. His conscientiousness was as great as his intuition. Klee achieved ultimate things because, though standing aloof from things, he was always ready to account for everything he did.

Klee

Niesen Landscape 1937

6 Conclusion

Klee died in 1940, during the war. In the postwar years his fame spread all over the world, but the younger generation was stimulated by his paintings, particularly the paintings of the years in Bern, rather than by his drawings. Few contemporary artists are great draftsmen. Among the older artists, there is Joan Miró, whose drawings breathe the spirit of Klee, and occasionally are as brilliant as his paintings. Miró was conquered by Klee's watercolors and drawings when he saw them for the first time in 1925 at the Surrealist exhibition in Paris. Miró's free lines and forms, as well as his humor, bring Klee to mind. Max Ernst was impressed by Klee's drawings in the 1920s; what linked him with Klee was his technical inventiveness (*Histoire naturelle*). But both Miró and Ernst were influenced by Klee before his death. Of the artists who became known after 1945, Wols (d. 1951) is the only one whose drawings remind us of Klee. Without imitating Klee, Wols combines formal and poetic elements into a pictorial whole. Like Klee, Wols was inspired by musical compositional techniques. He died too early to follow his path to the end and to prove the stimulating power of Klee's work.

The number of heirs of Klee the draftsman is small, smaller than the number of heirs of the painter. His painted work influences all schools of contemporary art, including the *tachistes*. His graphic work still awaits discovery; it is less known than his painted work and has not been effectively represented in the many Klee exhibitions. The drawings are kept in the portfolios of the Klee Foundation and the estate, in public print rooms, and in the cupboards of private collectors. Few art-lovers have time or opportunity to study them there at leisure. Klee has opened as many gates with his drawings as with his paintings. Someday they will be understood as road signs pointing to regions which Klee himself could not anticipate.

Specialfälle.

1) $a = 0$; gibt. $by + c = 0$; $y = -\dfrac{c}{b} = d$ (constant)

$y = d$ ist die Gl. einer Parallelen zur x-Achse im Abstande d von derselben.

$y = 0$;

2) $b = 0$; gibt $ax + c = 0$; $x = -\dfrac{c}{a} = $

$x = e$ ist die Gl. einer Parallelen zur y-Achse im Abstande e von derselben

$x = 0$ ist die Gl. der $y = $

3) $C = 0$

Page of Artist's Geometry Notebook   1898

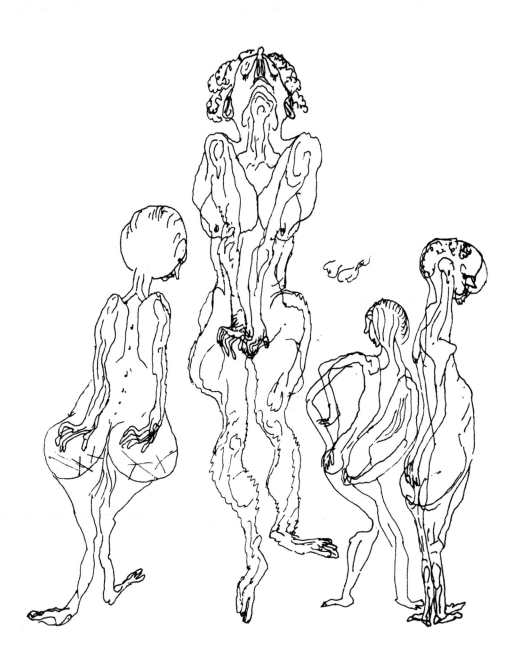

Four Nudes, Mother and Children Apprehensive over Father's Return 1908

54   *Friends Visiting a Sick Girl, 5 Figures*   *1909*

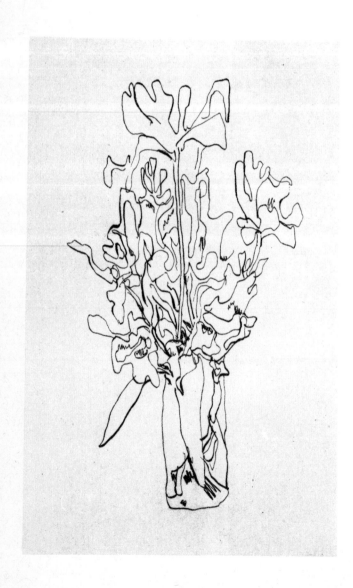

Buildings in Quarry at Ostermundigen near Bern   1909

Near Munich   1910   59

60   *Voltaire, Candide, Chap.15 "Place, place pour le révérend père colonel"*   *1911*

Street in Latin Quarter (near Place Saint-Michel) 1912

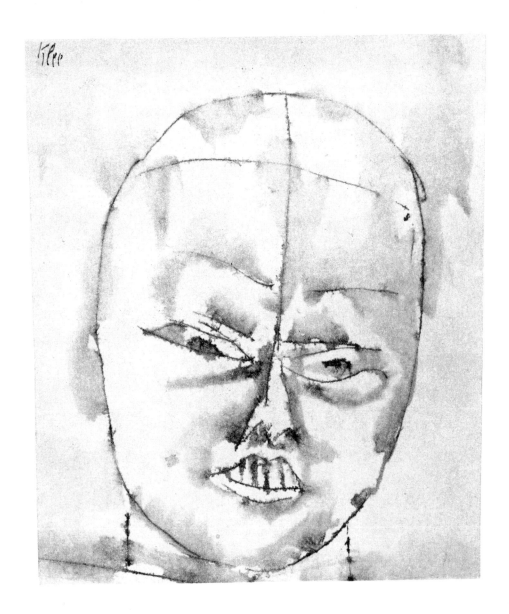

Jüngws Pierrot ——————————— 1912 99

64   *Horses Grazing*   *1912*

1913. 189. Fabelhafte Insel

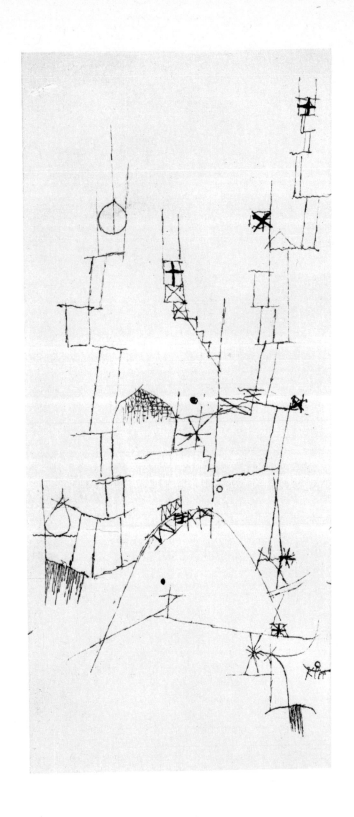

Jerusalem My Chief Joy   1914

Like a Stage Landscape *1917*

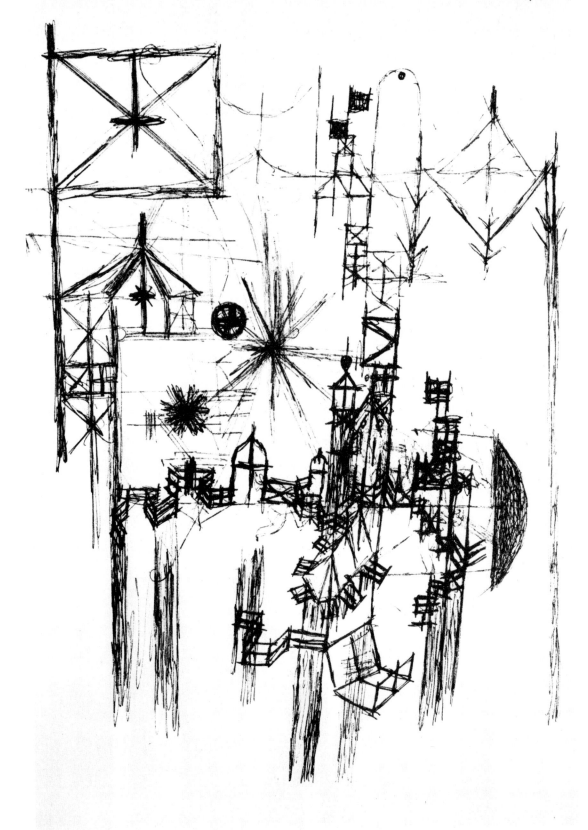

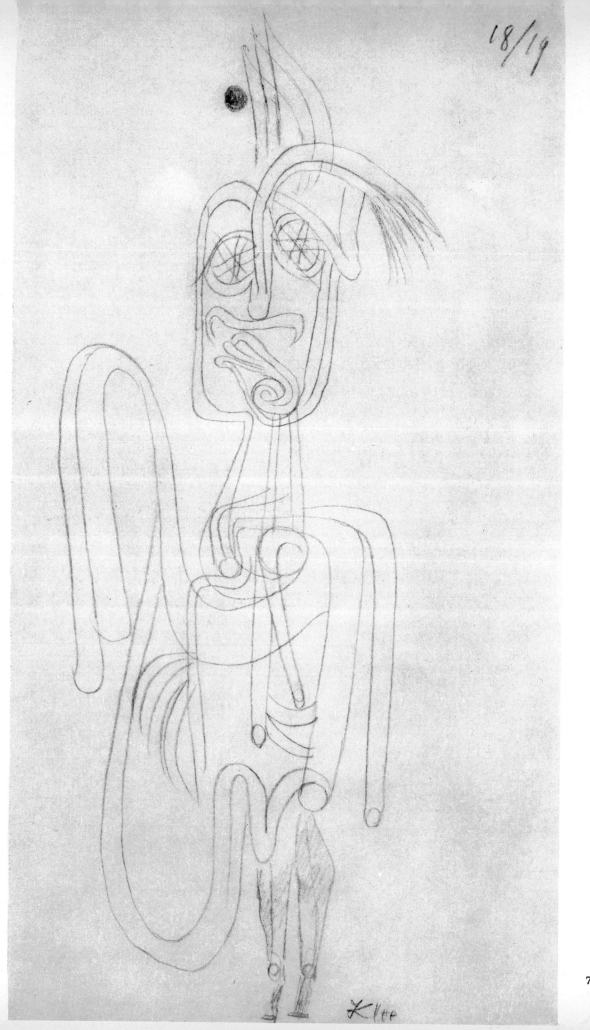

Klee

72   *Ghost of an Ancient Hero*   1918

Drawing with Fermata 1918   73

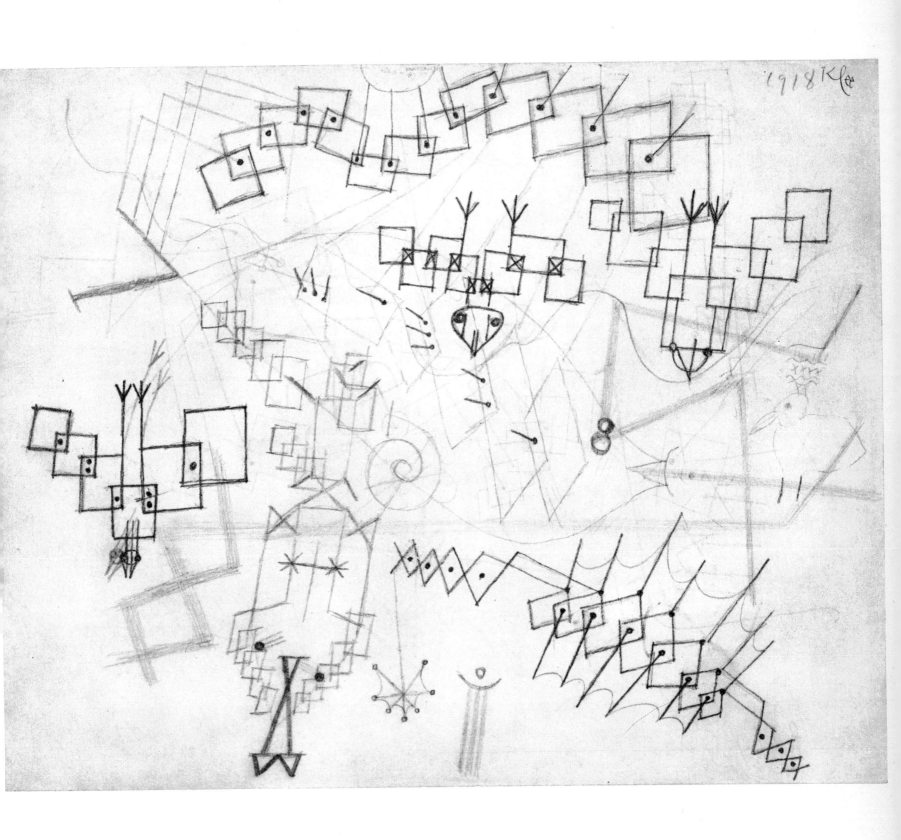

Bird Airplanes 1918 75

Ringing for Fish 1919

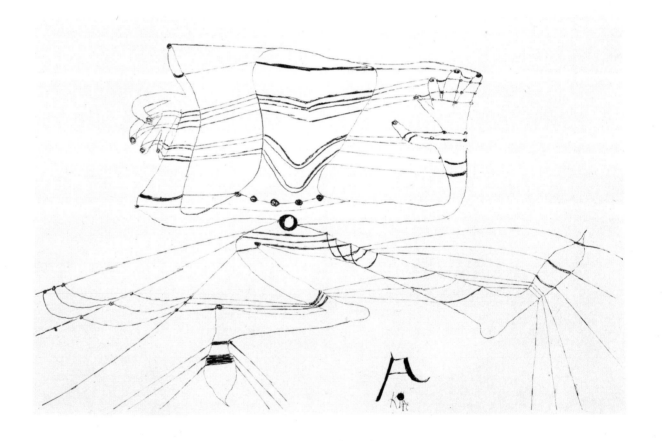

Concerning the Fate of Two Girls   1921

Drawing for "Star Container" **1921**

Drawing for "Dance You Monster to My Sweet Song" 1922   89

90   *Governess   1922*

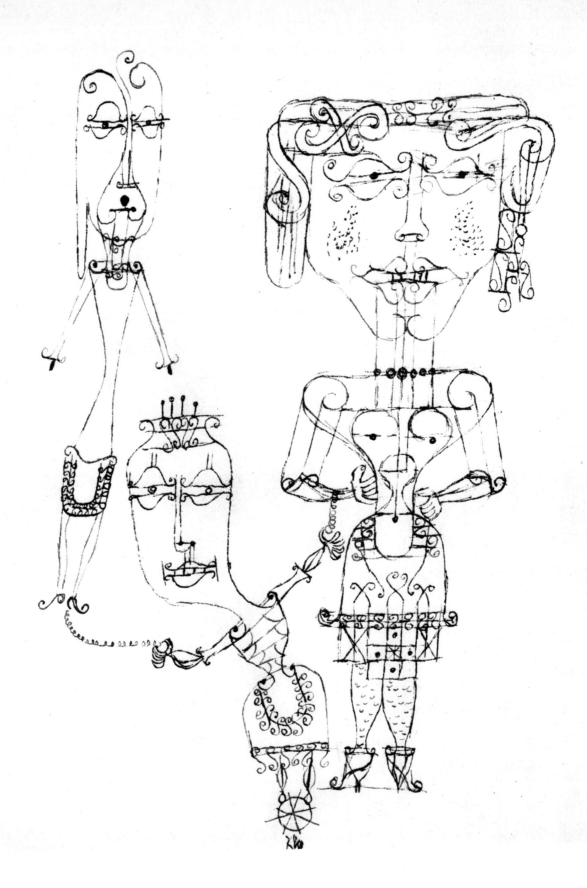

Portrait of an Expressionist 1922

94   *Physiognomy of a Dream*   1924

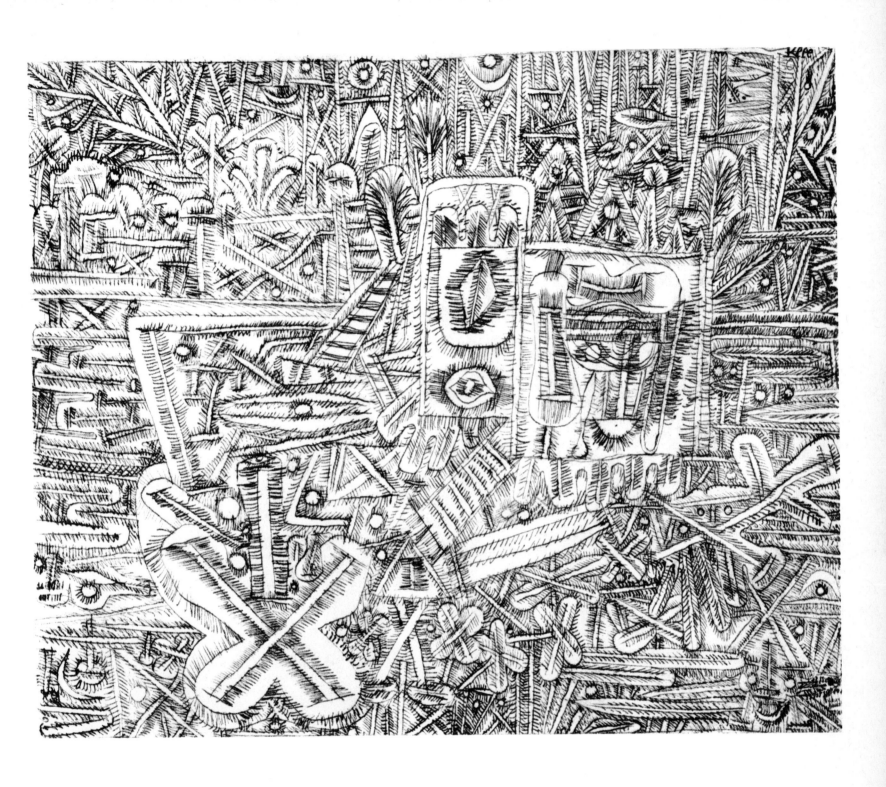

96   *Façade*   1924

Harlequin on Bridge 1923   97

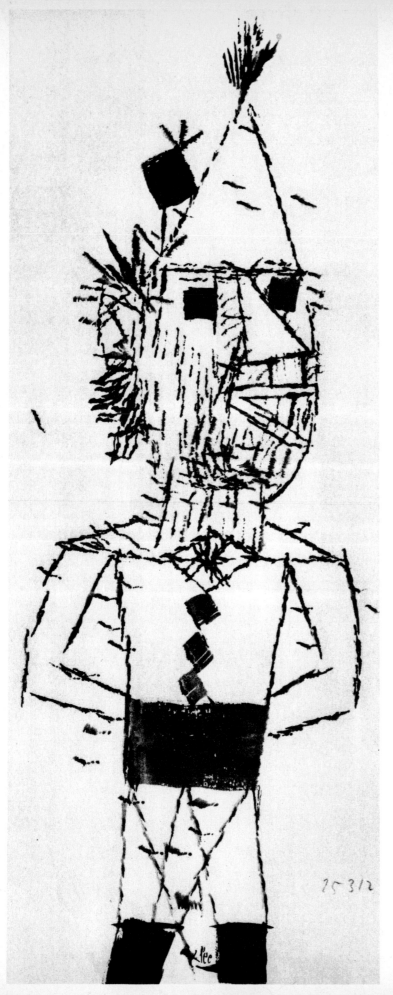

100   *Village Clown 1925*

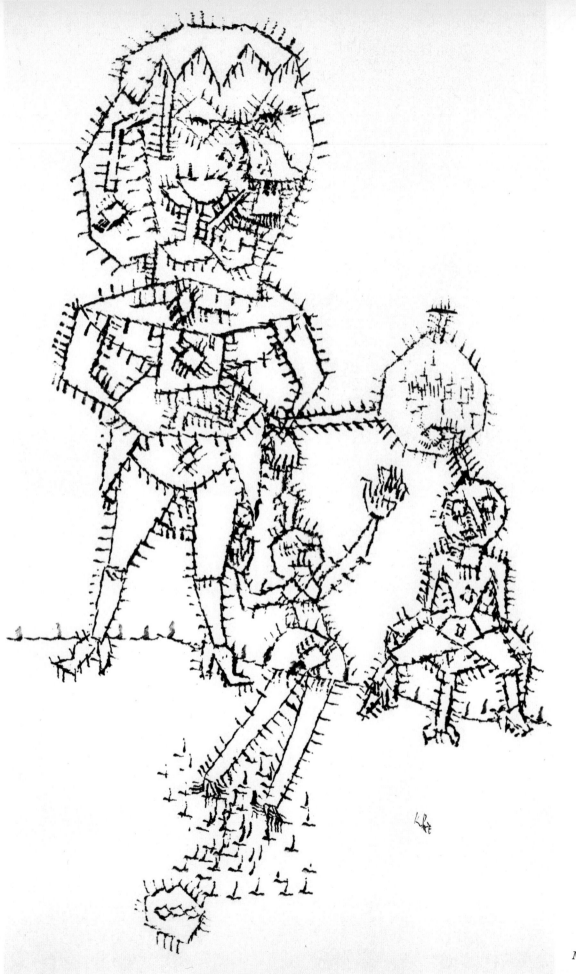

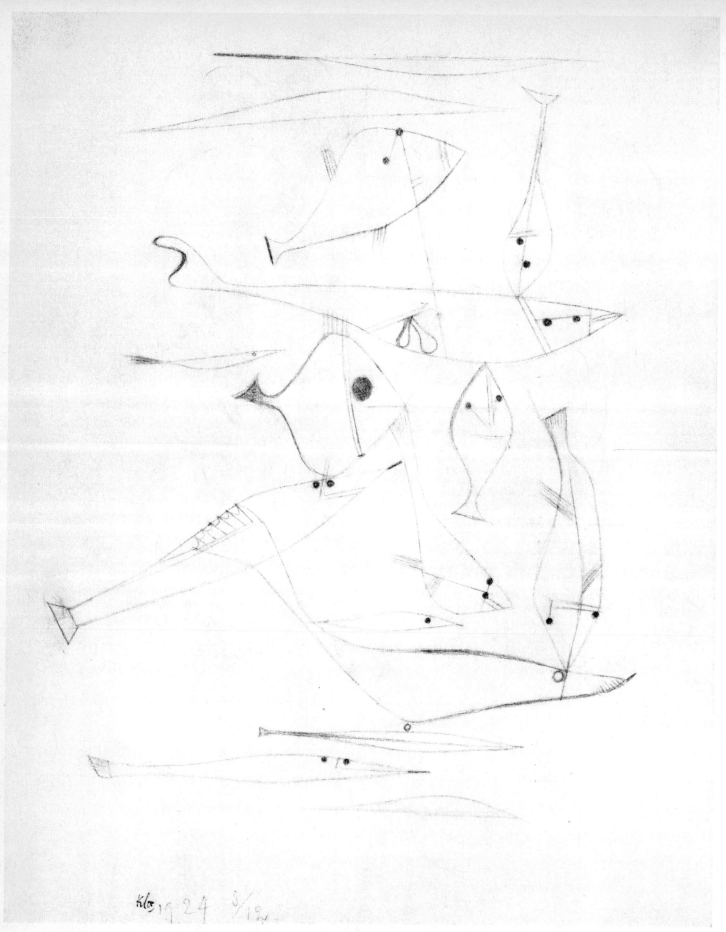

klee 1924 5/12

Second Drawing for Fish Picture   1924

Knowledge of an Animal   *1925*

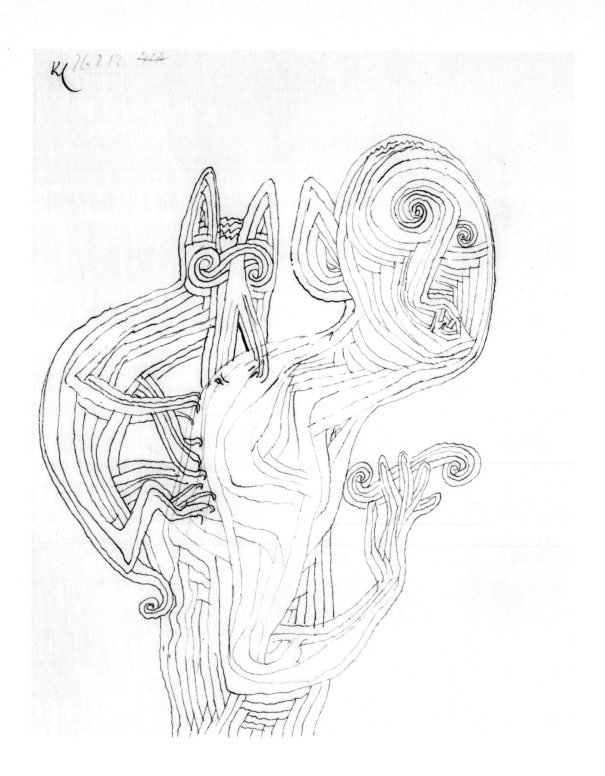

Bite on the Shoulder   1926

26412 Klee

Windmill Flowers 1926 109

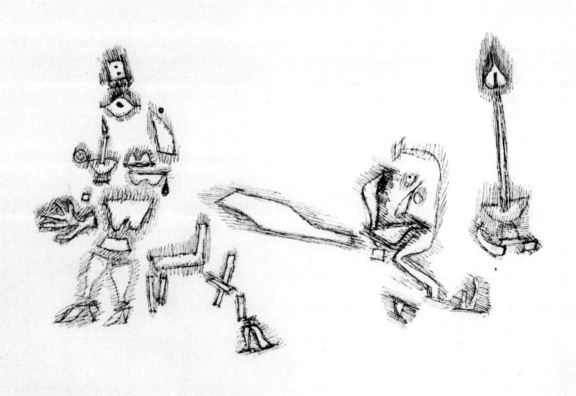

Houses in Flames   1929

Gathering Snowstorm (City and Atmosphere) 1927   119

grosser Circus

122   *Preaching to Animals in the Desert*   *1929*

124   *City Waterfront I*   1929

126   *Portrait of a Scholar   1930*

128   *Long Hair and Soulful   1929*

For the "Suppliants" 1932

Hamlet Maybe? 1932 133

134   *Lap Dog I*   1932

Waking from Dream 1932   135

Between Autumn and Winter 1932

138   *Experiment for Antigone 1933*

140   *A Poet Pregnant*   *1933*

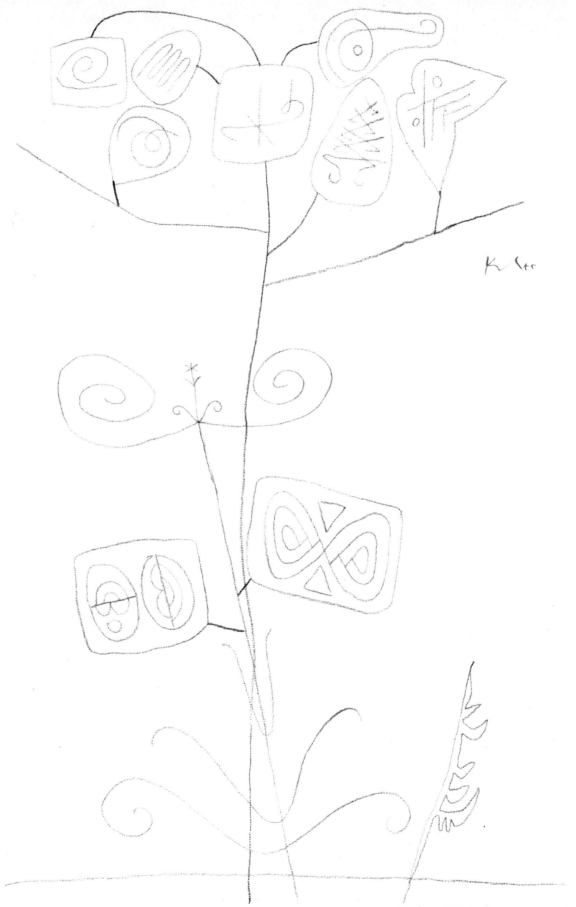

144   *Scene of Comical Riders 1935*

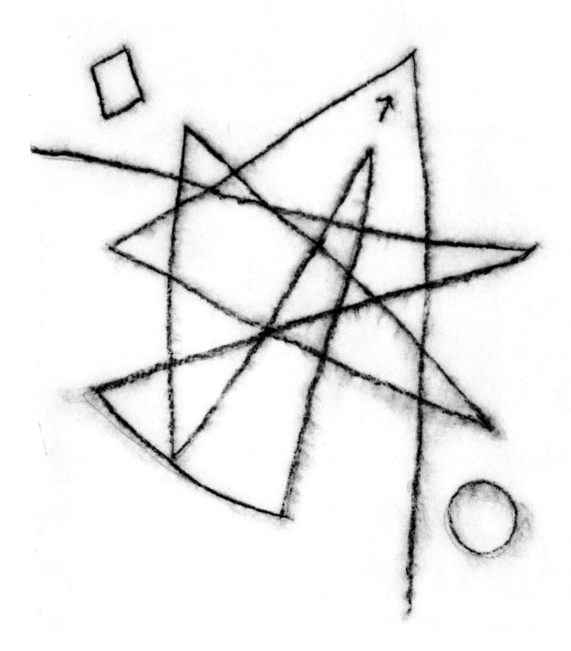

Stirrings of Growth *1938*

154   *Disgrace*   1939

Suis-je belle moi? 1939 155

156   *Railway Train*   *1939*

160   *Eidola: Former Pianist   1940*

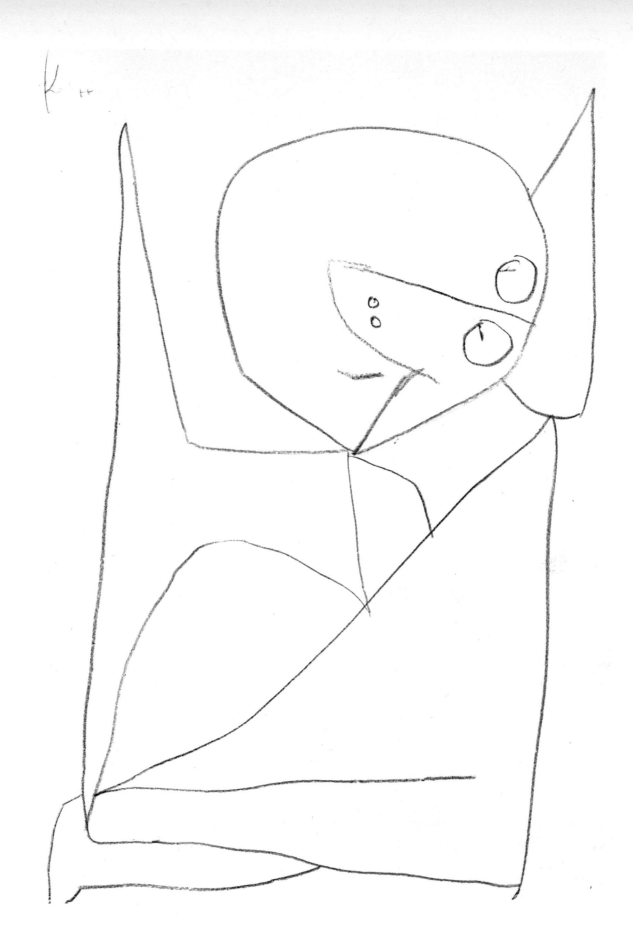

164   *Baptismal Font   1940*

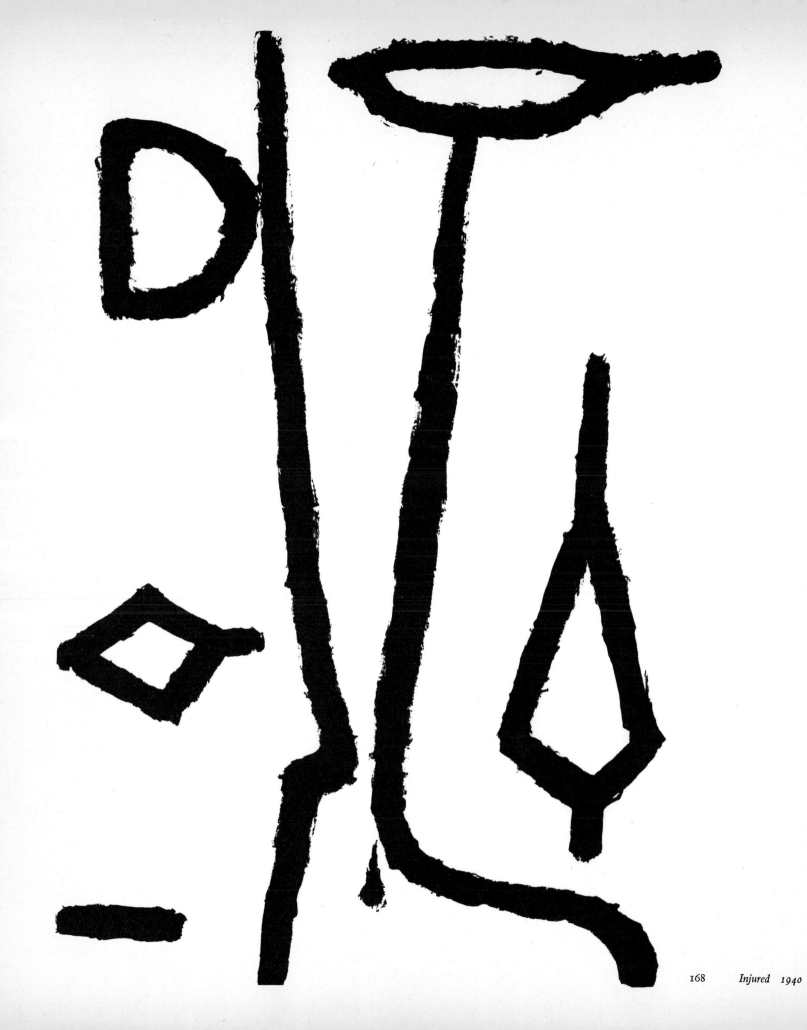

168   *Injured* 1940

Catalogue of Works Reproduced

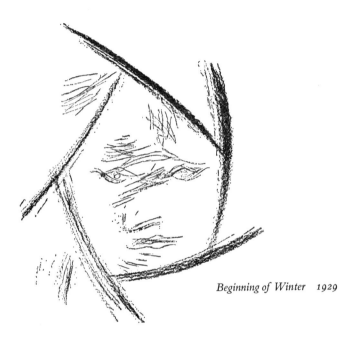

Beginning of Winter   1929

Data include the title, the year, the number in Klee's catalogue, notations of technique, dimensions, signature, owner, and the page where it is reproduced in this book.

From 1925 on, the catalogue number is followed by each year's serial number. All drawings are on paper, and were supplied with cardboard mountings by the artist. As a rule, the year and catalogue number together with the title are noted on the mounting below the drawing.

The titles used here are those supplied in Klee's catalogue; occasionally, different titles appear in the drawings.

The abbreviations l.l., u.l., l.r., r., u.r., c.r., b.c., l.c., t.c., t., mean, respectively, lower left, upper left, lower right, right, upper right, center right, bottom center, left center, top center, and top.

My Den. 1896. Not catalogued. Pen and wash. $3^5/_8 \times 5^7/_8$". "272 Paul Klee 15.11.96 Meine Bude" l. l. Klee Foundation, Bern. Page 49.

Page of Artist's Geometry Notebook. 1898. Not catalogued. Pen. $9 \times 7^1/_8$". Unsigned. Felix Klee, Bern. Page 50.

Man with Barrel Organ. 1905, No. 35. Pencil and wash. $6^3/_4 \times 3^1/_2$". "1905" u. l.; "Klee" l. l. Klee Foundation, Bern. Page 51.

Four Nudes, Mother and Children Apprehensive over Father's Return (Sketch for Comic Epic by Blösch). 1908, No. 3. Pen. $6^5/_8 \times 5^7/_8$". "Klee" u. l.; "1908, 3" l.l. Lady Nika Hulton, London. Page 52.

Two Aunts, Nudes with Bonnets. 1908, No. 14. Pen. $5^1/_2 \times 4^3/_4$". "Klee" u. l. Bernhard Sprengel, Hanover. Page 53.

Boy in Fur Coat. 1909, No. 4. Pen and wash (India ink). $9^1/_4 \times 8^7/_8$". "Klee 1909 4" l. r. G. David Thompson, Pittsburgh, Pa. Page 55.

Friends Visiting a Sick Girl, 5 Figures. 1909, No. 11. Pen and wash (India ink). $6^5/_8 \times 12^1/_4$". "Klee 1909" l. r. Klee Foundation, Bern. Page 54.

Buildings in Quarry at Ostermundigen near Bern. 1909, No. 60. Pen. $5^1/_2 \times 8^1/_8$". "Klee 1909" r. Formerly Curt Valentin, New York. Page 59.

Tidy Path in Woods near Bern. 1909, No. 62. India

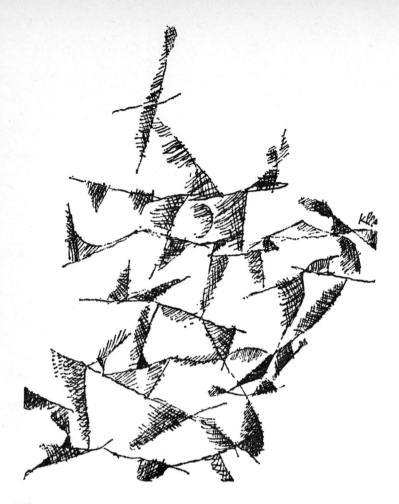

Flight to the Right, Abstract   1913

ink. 6³/₄×10¹/₈″. "Klee" l. r. Rolf and Kätti Bürgi, Bern. Page 57.

Tulips in Two Versions. 1910, No. 8. Left: 7¹/₈×4¹/₂″; right: 7¹/₈×5³/₈″. "Klee 1910" l. r. Galerie Rosengart, Lucerne. Page 58.

Near Munich, path at the left, little house with pointed tower top center, group of houses top right. 1910, No. 35. Pen. 4³/₈×8¹/₂″. "Klee" l. r. Angela Rosengart, Lucerne. Page 59.

Voltaire, Candide, Chap. 15 "Place, place pour le révérend père colonel." 1911, No. 80. Pen. 4³/₄×9″. "Klee" l. l. Klee Foundation, Bern. Page 60.

Head of a Young Pierrot. 1912, No. 99. Pen and brush on wet ground. 5⁵/₈×4⁷/₈″. "Klee" u. l. Rolf and Kätti Bürgi, Bern. Page 63.

Street in Latin Quarter (near Place Saint-Michel). 1912, No. 102. Pen and brush on wet ground. 4³/₄×4¹/₂″. "Klee" l. r. Felix Klee, Bern. Page 62.

Horses Grazing. 1912, No. 109. Black tempera and pen (grainy wash). 5⁷/₈×10¹/₈″. "Klee" l. r. F.C. Schang, New York. Page 64.

The Last Stage of Don Juan's Infatuation. 1913, No. 48. Pen. 3⁷/₈×9¹/₂″. "Klee" l. r. Klee Foundation, Bern. Page 61.

A Good Joke. 1913, No. 84. Pen. 5⁷/₈×4⁵/₈″. "Klee" u. r. Alex Vömel, Düsseldorf. Page 4.

Sketch for Portrait. 1913, No. 150. Black tempera and wash. 8×5″. "Klee" u. r. James Wise, Geneva. Page 65.

Flight to the Right, Abstract. 1913, No. 158. Pen. 5¹/₂×4¹/₈″. "Klee" c. r. Klee Foundation, Bern. Page 170.

Song of Lamentation. 1913, No. 163. Pen. "Klee" l. r. Formerly Galerie Berggruen, Paris. Page 67.

Fabulous Island. 1913, No. 189. Pen. $2^3/_8 \times 7^5/_8$". "Klee" l. l. Klee Foundation, Bern. Page 66.

Sketch from Kairouan. 1914, No. 46. Pen. $6^1/_4 \times 3^1/_8$". "Klee" u. r. Klee Foundation, Bern. Page 8.

Jerusalem My Chief Joy. 1914, No. 161. Pen. $7^1/_2 \times 3^1/_4$". "Klee" l. r. Siegfried Rosengart, Lucerne. Page 68.

Untitled (like a vignette). 1915, No. 215. Pen. $7^5/_8 \times 5^3/_8$". "Klee" b. c. Bernhard Sprengel, Hanover. Page 69.

Like a Stage Landscape. 1917, No. 19. Pencil. $3^3/_4 \times 5^5/_8$". Klee Foundation, Bern. Page 70.

Drawing for Evil Star of Ships (d. for 1919, No. 90). 1917, No. 152. Pen. $8^3/_8 \times 10^3/_4$". "Klee" u. l. Klee Foundation, Bern. Frontispiece.

With the Flag. 1918, No. 6. Pen. $8^5/_8 \times 5^1/_2$". "Klee" u. r. Collection John Lefèbre, Paris. Page 71.

Two Acrobats on a Ladder with a Heart (title on cardboard mounting is *Scherzo on Ladder* b. c.). 1918, No. 174. Pen. $11^1/_2 \times 8^3/_4$". "1918, 174" l. l.; "Klee" somewhat higher. Private collection, U.S.A. Page 21.

Ghost of an Ancient Hero. 1918, No. 203. Pencil. $10^1/_2 \times 5^7/_8$". "Klee" b. c. Klee Foundation, Bern. Page 72.

Drawing with Fermata. 1918, No. 209. Pen. $6^1/_4 \times 9^1/_2$". "Klee" u. r. Klee Foundation, Bern. Page 73.

Bird Airplanes. 1918, No. 210. Pencil. $8^1/_2 \times 10^3/_4$". "1918 Klee" u. r. Felix Klee, Bern. Page 75.

Artist Pondering. 1919, No. 73. Transfer. $7^5/_8 \times 6^1/_2$". "Klee" u. r. Felix Klee, Bern. Page 77.

Ringing for Fish. 1919, No. 228. Pen. $8^5/_8 \times 11$". "Klee" l. r. Formerly Galerie Berggruen, Paris. Page 76.

Celebrating the Arrival of the New Ships. 1919, No. 265. Pen. $6^1/_2 \times 8^5/_8$". "Klee 1919" u. l. Eleanor Saidenberg, New York. Page 79.

Composition on Parallel Horizontals. 1920, No. 63. Pencil. $7^3/_8 \times 11^1/_8$". "Klee" l. r. Galerie Rosengart, Lucerne. Page 78.

Dance of the Veils (d. for 1920/34). 1920, No. 66. Pen. $7^1/_4 \times 10^3/_4$". "Klee" b. c. Private collection, Munich. Page 80.

Black Magician (d. for 1920-13). 1920, No. 70. Pencil. 11×9". "Klee" l. l. Angela Rosengart, Lucerne. Page 81.

Park on Lake (without Houses). 1920, No. 102. Wash drawing. $6^7/_8 \times 8^3/_4$". "Klee" u. r. Felix Klee, Bern. Page 83.

Comedy (d. for 1921/108). 1921, No. 109. Pen. Left side: $8^3/_4 \times 6^1/_8$"; right side: $8^3/_4 \times 5$". "Klee" u. l. (left side). Galerie Rosengart, Lucerne. Page 85.

Concerning the Fate of Two Girls. 1921, No. 112. Oil drawing. 8⁵/₈ × 11¹/₄″. "Klee" u. r. Bernhard Sprengel, Hanover. Page 84.

Drawing for "Occupied Room in Perspective" (d. for 1920/24). 1921, No. 168. Pencil. 13⁷/₈ × 9³/₄″. "Klee" t. Klee Foundation, Bern. Page 87.

Drawing for "Star Container" (d. for 1922/130). 1921, No. 194. Pen. 8¹/₈ × 10³/₄″. "Klee" u. r. Rolf and Kätti Bürgi, Bern. Page 88.

Drawing for "Dance You Monster to My Sweet Song" (d. for 1922/54). 1922, No. 55. Pen. 13¹/₂ × 10¹/₄″. "Klee" u. l. Siegfried Rosengart, Lucerne. Page 89.

Costumed Puppets. 1922, No. 85. Pen. 9³/₈ × 6⁵/₈″. "Klee" b. c. S. R. Guggenheim Museum, New York. Page 91.

Governess. 1922, No. 214. Pencil. 11¹/₄ × 8³/₄″. "Klee 1922" u. l. Siegfried Rosengart, Lucerne. Page 90.

Equipment for Advanced Acrobatics. 1922, No. 234. Pencil. 11 × 8¹/₄″. "Klee" u. l. Private collection, U.S.A. Page 23.

Portrait of an Expressionist. 1922, No. 240. Brush. 12¹/₈ × 8³/₄″. "Klee" u. r. Jane Wade, New York. Page 92.

Fashion Picture (à la classique). (d. for 1922/91). 1922, No. 256. Pen. 8³/₄ × 11″. "1922 Klee" u. l. Angela Rosengart, Lucerne. Page 93.

Harlequin on Bridge. 1923, No. 78. Oil drawing, black. "Klee" u. r. Galerie Berggruen, Paris. Page 97.

Still Life of Bazaar. 1924, No. 28. Pen (violet ink). 7¹/₄ × 8⁷/₈″. "Klee" u. r. H. Berggruen, Paris. Page 95.

Physiognomy of a Dream. 1924, No. 83. Pencil. 11 × 9″. "Klee" u. l. Clifford Odets, Beverly Hills, Calif. Page 94.

Façade. 1924, No. 171. Pen on wet ground. 10¹/₄ × 12¹/₈″· "Klee" l. l. Private collection, New York. Page 96.

Oriental Girl. 1924, No. 256. Oil drawing tinted with a spray. 11³/₄ × 9¹/₈″. "Klee" b. c. Siegfried Rosengart, Lucerne. Page 99.

First Drawing for Fish Picture (d. for 1925/5). 1924, No. 279. Pencil. 11¹/₈ × 9″. "Klee" u.r. Collection unknown. Page 175.

Second Drawing for Fish Picture (d. for 1925/5). 1924, No. 280. 11 × 8⁷/₈″. "Klee 1924" b. c. Angela Rosengart, Lucerne. Page 102.

Mother of Witches. 1925, L 1, No. 21. Wide brush. 9¹/₄ × 5¹/₂″. "Klee" l. r. Clifford Odets, Beverly Hills, Calif. Page 101.

Village Clown. 1925, n 7, No. 47. Wide brush. 10¹/₄ × 4¹/₈″. "Klee" b. c. F. C. Schang, New York. Page 100.

Village with Sunflowers. 1925, h 2, No. 172. Pen. 5¹/₂ × 9⁵/₈″. "Klee" l. r. Bernhard Sprengel, Hanover. Page 103.

Knowledge of an Animal. 1925, t zero, No. 190. Pen. 12⁵/₈×8¹/₂″. "Klee" u. l. Busch-Reisinger Museum, Cambridge, Mass. Page 106.

View of a Mountain Shrine. 1926, k 8, No. 18. Watercolor and pen. 18¹/₂×11³/₄″. "Klee" l. r. Bernhard Sprengel, Hanover. Page 105.

Bite on the Shoulder. 1926, n 5, No. 45. Pen. 7¹/₈×5⁷/₈″. "Klee" u. l. Galerie Rosengart, Lucerne. Page 108.

Windmill Flowers. 1926, c zero, No. 120. Pencil. 10³/₄× 8³/₄″. "Klee" u. r. Felix Klee, Bern. Page 109.

Snake with Prey. 1926, v 1, No. 211. Pen (India ink). 9³/₈×12¹/₂″. "Klee" l. c. Formerly Galerie Berggruen, Paris. Page 107.

The Great Dome. 1927, n 3, No. 43. Pen. 10¹/₂×12″. "Klee" l. l. Klee Foundation, Bern. Page 10.

Port of Plit. 1927, q 7, No. 75. Reed pen. 12¹/₂×18³/₄″. "Klee" l. l. Formerly Galerie Berggruen, Paris. Page 111.

Frightened Ships. 1927, q 7, No. 77. Reed pen. 12¹/₂ ×18¹/₄″. "Klee" u. l. Felix Klee, Bern. Page 110.

Dutch Cathedral. 1927, r 4, No. 84. Reed pen. 11⁷/₈×18³/₈″. "Klee" u. r. Formerly Galerie Berggruen, Paris. Page 113.

Ship on Course. 1927, b 4, No. 114. Carbon-paper tracing. 12¹/₄×9¹/₂″. "Klee" l. l. Felix Klee, Bern. Page 30.

Constructive Play. 1927, b 5, No. 115. Carbon-paper tracing. 9³/₈×12¹/₈″. "Klee" u. r. Private collection, U.S.A. Page 1.

Accomplished. 1927, f 7, No. 153. Steel pen. 9³/₄×18″. "Klee" l. r. Collection unknown. Page 112.

Little Fool in Trance. 1927, g 10, No. 170. Oil drawing. 18¹/₄×12″. "Klee" l. l. Siegfried Rosengart, Lucerne. Page 115.

Would Should. 1927, z 7, No. 257. Pen. 11³/₈×17⁵/₈″. "Klee" u. l. Collection unknown. Page 114.

What a Mess You've Made! 1927, z 10, No. 260. Pen. 12×9³/₄″. "Klee" t. c. Rolf and Kätti Bürgi, Bern. Page 117.

Losing Control. 1927, ae 2, No. 262. Pen. 12¹/₄×6″. "Klee" u. r. Formerly Gallery Curt Valentin, New York. Page 116.

Toys. 1927, oe 1, No. 271. Pen. 3×11¹/₄″. "Klee" u. r. Galerie Otto Stangl, Munich. Page 35.

Gathering Snowstorm (City and Atmosphere). 1927, omega 1, No. 291. Watercolor and pen. 21¹/₂×12¹/₄″. "Klee" u. l. National Gallery of Scotland, Edinburgh. Page 119.

Excitement Before Trip. 1927, 3 h 4, No. 304. Pen. 11³/₄ ×12″. "Klee" t. c. F. C. Schang, New York. Page 14.

Two Blossoms. 1927, 3 h 15, No. 315. Pen. 11³/₄×9¹/₄″. "Klee" u. l. Collection unknown. Page 31.

Big Circus. 1928, L 2, No. 22. Pen. 17³/₄×12″. "Klee" l.; "Grosser Circus" b. c. Rolf and Kätti Bürgi, Bern. Page 121.

Houses in Flames. 1929, r 2, No. 82. Grease crayon. 12⁷/₈×8¹/₈″. "Klee" u. r. Felix Klee, Bern. Page 118.

Beginning of Winter. 1929, b 10, No. 120. Grease crayon. 11¹/₄×9³/₄″. Collection unknown. Page 169.

Preaching to Animals in the Desert. 1929, t 7, No. 197. Greasy chalk. 17³/₄×23³/₈″. "Klee" u. r. Siegfried Rosengart, Lucerne. Page 122.

Nomad Prince. 1929, t 9, No. 199. Greasy chalk. 12×17³/₄″. "Klee" b. c. Klee Foundation, Bern. Page 123.

City Waterfront I. 1929, u 2, No. 202. Red and violet greasy chalk. 12⁷/₈×8¹/₈″. "Klee" u. r. Felix Klee, Bern. Page 124.

Long Hair and Soulful. 1929, om 9, No. 299. Pen. 11¹/₄×9″. "Klee" u. r. F. C. Schang, New York. Page 128.

Dreamy. 1930, r 1, No. 81. Pen. 9⁷/₈×12″. "Klee" b. c. Klee Foundation, Bern. Page 26.

Further Study in Three Dimensions. 1930, v 7, No. 117. Charcoal rubbing. 13¹/₂×18¹/₈″. "Klee" l. l. Felix Klee, Bern. Page 125.

Portrait of a Scholar. 1930, s 6, No. 216. Brush drawing with stencils. 19¹/₂×14″. "Klee" u. l. M. H. Drey, London. Page 126.

Reflective Wanderer. 1931, k 10, No. 30. Reed pen. 16³/₄×20″. "Klee" l. r. Collection unknown. Page 129.

Old Maid. 1931, L 6, No. 46. Pen. 18⁷/₈×12¹/₂″. "Klee" l. r. Felix Klee, Bern. Page 127.

Under the Angel's Wing on a Steep Path. 1931, L 17, No. 57. Pen. 22×17³/₈″. "Klee" l. r. Klee Foundation, Bern. Page 131.

Successful Adventure. 1931, q 16, No. 136. Pen (India ink). 11¹/₂×20¹/₈″. "Klee" l. l. Rolf and Kätti Bürgi, Bern. Page 37.

For the "Suppliants." 1932, r 3, No. 143. Pen. 7¹/₂×6³/₈″. "Klee" l. l. Klee Foundation, Bern. Page 130.

Before the Temple. 1932, r 15, No. 155. Heavy pencil. 12¹/₈×12¹/₂″. "Klee" l. l. Felix Klee, Bern. Page 132.

Lap Dog I. 1932, s 16, No. 176. Charcoal. 18³/₄×24³/₄″. "Klee" l. l. Klee Foundation, Bern. Page 134.

Hamlet Maybe? 1932, y 17, No. 297. Brush drawing. 10³/₄×5¹/₂″. "Klee" u. l. Felix Klee, Bern. Page 133.

Waking from Dream. 1932, z 4, No. 304. Brush drawing 12¹/₂×16³/₄″. "Klee" t. c. Klee Foundation, Bern. Page 135.

Between Autumn and Winter. 1932, z 16, No. 316. Brush drawing. 20×14¹/₄″. "Klee" l. r. Klee Foundation, Bern. Page 136.

Frost. 1932, a 20, No. 340. Pen. 16³/₄×12¹/₂″. "Klee" u.l. Felix Klee, Bern. Page 137.

Experiment for Antigone. 1933, L 15, No. 35. Brush drawing. 24¹/₄×18⁷/₈″. "Klee" u.l. Klee Foundation, Bern. Page 138.

Exit. 1933, t 5, No. 165. Heavy pencil. 12⁷/₈×8¹/₄″. "Klee" t. c. Rolf and Kätti Bürgi, Bern. Page 139.

What a Proposal! 1933, a 19, No. 319. Heavy pencil. 10¹/₈×10³/₄″. "Klee" l. r. Felix Klee, Bern. Page 141.

A Poet Pregnant. 1933, b 20, No. 340. Pencil. 17¹/₂×10¹/₂″. "Klee" l. r. Klee Foundation, Bern. Page 140.

Diary Port Cros: South Coast, Porquerolles in the Distance. 1933, i 14, No. 474. Pencil. 16¹/₂×11³/₄″. "Klee" u. r. Felix Klee, Bern. Page 142.

Wavy Leaf. 1934, N 13, No. 93. Pencil. 12×18³/₄″. "Klee" u. r. Mies van der Rohe, Chicago. Page 42.

Diagram of the Redemption. 1934, P 16, No. 116. Pencil. 18⁷/₈×12¹/₄″. "Klee" u. r. Felix Klee, Bern. Page 44.

Enforced Outcome. 1934, P 19, No. 119. Red chalk. 16³/₈×12¹/₄″. "Klee" t. c. Felix Klee, Bern. Page 145.

Symbiosis (Botanical). 1934, Qu 11, No. 131. Pencil. 18³/₄×12¹/₂″. "Klee" u. r. Felix Klee, Bern. Page 143.

Scene of Comical Riders. 1935, M 12, No. 72. Heavy pencil. 16¹/₂×11³/₈″. "Klee" u. l. Private collection, U.S.A. Page 144.

Oh Dear! 1937, U 1, No. 201. Black watercolor and paste color. 11×7″. "Klee" l. r. Rolf and Kätti Bürgi, Bern. Page 147.

Niesen Landscape. 1937, V ii, No. 231. Black paste color. 12×10³/₄″. "Klee" u. r. Galerie Otto Stangl, Munich. Page 46.

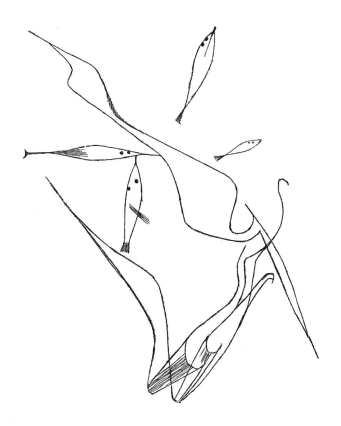

First Drawing for Fish Picture 1924

Little Runaway. 1937, V 15, No. 235. Black paste color. $18^3/_4 \times 12^7/_8''$. "Klee" l. l. Max Bill, Zurich. Page 146.

Stirrings of Growth. 1938, F 18, No. 78. Black paste color. $12^7/_8 \times 19''$. "Klee" u. l. Felix Klee, Bern. Page 148.

Canal Locks. 1938, M 6, No. 186. Heavy pencil. $3^5/_8 \times 15^1/_8''$. "Klee" u. l. Felix Klee, Bern. Page 17.

Alphabet II. 1938, M 8, No. 188. Brush drawing (black watercolor). $19^1/_2 \times 12^7/_8''$. "Klee" u. r. Klee Foundation, Bern. Page 149.

Vegetation. 1938, R 6, No. 266. Black watercolor. $10^1/_2 \times 8^3/_8''$. "Klee" l. r. Klee Foundation, Bern. Page 151.

Child and Phantom. 1938, Y 6, No. 406. Black paste color, brush. $26^3/_4 \times 19''$. "Klee" u. r. and l. c. Bernhard Sprengel, Hanover. Page 153.

A Nest, Its Coat-of-Arms, Its Future. 1938, C 2, No. 482. Pen. $11^3/_4 \times 8^1/_4''$. "Klee" r. Frankfurter Kunstkabinett. Page 150.

Disgrace. 1939, AA 14, No. 514. Pencil. $11^3/_4 \times 8^1/_8''$. "Klee" u. r. Klee Foundation, Bern. Page 154.

Railway Train. 1939, FF 9, No. 609. Pencil. $10^1/_2 \times 16^3/_4''$. "Klee" u. r. Klee Foundation, Bern. Page 156.

Suis-je belle moi? 1939, KK 9, No. 689. Pencil. $10^1/_2 \times 8^1/_2''$. "Klee" u. r. Klee Foundation, Bern. Page 155.

Rock of Angels. 1939, UU 7, No. 847. Pencil. $11^5/_8 \times 8^1/_4''$. "Klee" u. l. Klee Foundation, Bern. Page 157.

Hopeful Angel (Physiognomic). 1939, WW 12, No. 892. Pencil. $11^1/_2 \times 8^1/_8''$. "Klee" l. l. Klee Foundation, Bern. Page 159.

Angel's Crisis I. 1939, DE 1, No. 1021. Heavy pencil. $16^1/_2 \times 11^1/_2''$. "Klee" u. l. Felix Klee, Bern. Page 161.

Eidola: Former Pianist. 1940, U 4, No. 104. Heavy pencil. $11^5/_8 \times 8^1/_4''$. "Klee" l. r. Klee Foundation, Bern. Page 160.

Family Quarrel. 1940, U 10, No. 110. Heavy pencil. $8^1/_4 \times 11^1/_4''$. "Klee" l. l. Felix Klee, Bern. Page 162.

Torch Bearer. 1940, S 10, No. 150. Pen, ink. $11^5/_8 \times 8^1/_8''$. "Klee" l. l. Felix Klee, Bern. Page 163.

Passion: Dürer's Mother, Too. 1940, R 18, No. 178. Heavy pencil. $11^1/_2 \times 8^1/_4''$. "Klee" l. l. Klee Foundation, Bern. Page 165.

Baptismal Font. 1940, Qu 11, No. 191. Heavy pencil. $11^1/_2 \times 8^5/_8''$. "Klee" l. l. Klee Foundation, Bern. Page 164.

Through Poseidon. 1940, P 19, No. 219. Pen, ink. $8 \times 11^5/_8''$. "Klee" l. r. David G. Thompson, Pittsburgh. Page 41.

Injured. 1940, H 16, No. 316. Black paste color. $16^1/_4 \times 11^1/_2''$. "Klee" u. l. Klee Foundation, Bern. Page 168.

They All Run After! 1940, G 5, No. 325. Black paste color. $12^5/_8 \times 16^3/_4''$. "Klee" u. l. Klee Foundation, Bern. Page 167.